Managing
Change in
the Workplace

For Chris and Jessica, with love,
and in memory of David.

Managing Change in the Workplace

New Approaches to Employee Relations

ALAN CAVE

Coopers
&Lybrand

KOGAN
PAGE

First published in 1994

Kogan Page Limited
120 Pentonville Road
London N1 9JN

British Library Cataloguing in Publication Data

A CIP record for this book is available from the British Library.

ISBN 0 7494 1007 8

Typeset by DP Photosetting, Aylesbury, Bucks
Printed in England by Clays Ltd, St Ives plc

Contents

Acknowledgements

I owe a huge debt of gratitude to many people for all the help I have received whilst writing this book.

I must first of all thank the Master and Fellows of Pembroke College, Oxford, whose decision to grant me the Ward-Perkins visiting fellowship in 1992 made possible the whole enterprise. That possibility became a practical reality due to the support of Roger Cooke, and of Margaret Exley and my new colleagues at Kinsley Lord.

Throughout the process of thinking, talking, arguing, writing and rewriting I have had the best support I could possibly have asked for. First and foremost I have enjoyed (in every sense!) the advice, wit, wisdom and companionship of Ceri Thomas and Paul Willman, (at its best over a few pints at the Turk's Head), without whom I should never have got going or kept going.

Philip Bassett gave me a much needed shove at a crucial moment and has commented helpfully and generously on successive drafts, as well as being throughout a source of great knowledge, sound judgement and free thinking. Ken Mayhew and Derek Robinson from Oxford, friends and mentors for half a lifetime, have been generous in the time and advice that they have given me over the course of the last two years. And Michael Armstrong has excelled as a supportive commissioning editor – ever helpful and encouraging in his comments and guidance – supported in his task, (which must have felt at times like trying to herd squirrels), by Kelvin Hard and by Pauline Goodwin, who couldn't have been kinder or more helpful.

John Monks and his colleagues at the TUC provided an excellent opportunity to test out some of the ideas in Chapter 8 with them in a wide ranging, thoughtful and good natured session. Ray Dickens of Air Products and Ray Fletcher of H&R Johnson were extremely helpful in explaining the changes, and the context for those changes, within their companies in recent years. Paul Marginson and Anne-Marie Southall helped me to find the right focus in the early stages of writing and commented constructively on early drafts. Those drafts were made possible by the help and forebearence of Marie Tewkesbury, who proved that it is possible to produce a genuinely idiot-proof guide to word processing!

Above all I shall remain eternally grateful for a lifetime of support from my father and mother, Bernard and Joan Cave, and for the love and understanding of Chris and Jessica, who have put up with a lot and have never wavered in their support while I've been tapping away on this. The dedication at the front of the book is heartfelt.

CHAPTER 1

Introduction

POINTS OF DEPARTURE

The world of work of the 1990s is a very different place from that of 15 years ago. Over the last decade we have seen a sea change in the way people are managed. The relationship between employer and employee, the contractual basis on which it is carried out, the institutions which surround it – and indeed the bigger question of how the management of people as a resource is seen to fit in with the conduct of business as a whole – all these have been through a series of transformations.

I set out to write a book that took stock of where we have come to as a result of all this change. I wanted to look 'top down', at what senior managers are trying to achieve through the management of their employees – at their mental models of 'successful' people management and employee relations, and at how this area of management fits into the wider scheme of things. And I wanted to look 'bottom up', at the experience of those on the receiving end of all the change. What does it feel like? Does it make any kind of coherent sense? What is the every-day reality behind the management talk of 'new ways'?

Putting these two aspects together the central question is this: is British business now better at managing people?

I also wanted to take both an internal and an external perspective. By 'internal' I mean a focus on the internal concerns and thinking of organisations: the way in which they organise and shape their resources in response to outside forces and the way in which they evolve their strategies and then translate them into organisational practice, management styles and employment behaviour.

The 'external' focus concerns the macro consequences of all these local internal decisions. What does it all mean for 'UK plc'? Is the net effect to produce a more competitive economy, a labour market that is more efficient, a population that is more highly skilled, a better place to live and work?

Throughout the preparation and writing of the book I found myself returning time and again to a core list of questions on which I wanted to throw more light:

- Are people now being managed more effectively and productively?
- Are labour markets working more efficiently in their more deregulated state?
- Have the new stress on individualism and the new approaches to human resource management improved the position of people at work?
- What does all this change feel like for those on the receiving end: something positive, or a case of 'meet the new boss, the same as the old boss'?

ASSUMPTIONS AND PREJUDICES

We all have our own assumptions, prejudices and mental baggage. It's only fair that I should be as explicit as possible about mine. A working life divided more or less evenly between years spent in the world of trade unions and industrial relations and years spent as a management consultant have left me with some core beliefs that you will find popping up at regular intervals.

A sense of delight, for example, at finding good managers bringing out the best in their staff and helping to realise their potential and produce good business results; a corresponding (and more frequent) depression when confronted with managerial ineptness that results in under-achievement and the impoverishment of working life. A persisting belief in the positive role that trade unions *can* play in the workplace if they get their act together and understand the needs of employer and employee alike; and a frequent frustration at the sight of unions getting it badly wrong.

Above all perhaps there is a tenacious attachment to the notion of *pluralism*, in management and the world of work as much as in political life: a belief that respect for, and tolerance of, difference and non-conformity is not just a humane and civilised value but that it also offers the best chance of producing efficient outcomes.

I am using the term 'pluralism' here in the following sense:

- Different groups compete and bargain for a share of power and influence
- The diversity of different interests is recognised, along with the legitimate right of individuals and groups to represent those interests.
- The organisation is seen as a plurality of power holders, drawing their power from a variety of sources.
- A successful outcome is the negotiation of an agreed order involving compromise all round, which creates unity out of diversity.

This is to be contrasted with the idea of 'unitarism' – the belief that:

- The organisation is united under the umbrella of common goals and strives towards them like a well-integrated team.
- Disagreement and conflict are unhealthy – the sign of weak management and the presence of troublemakers.
- The role of management is to articulate, lead and enforce the 'common interest'.

So, a recurring theme concerns the extent to which the pluralism on which much of the traditional British approach to employee relations rested – with its emphasis on agreements between two 'sides' and on operating within jointly-agreed procedures – has been superseded, and the consequences of this.

Are we now living in a post-pluralist business world? If so, does it matter? Is it true, as some argue, that doing away with the essential features of pluralism – negotiation, the search for agreement, the building of consensus – undermines performance and produces second-best outcomes? Or is it rather the reverse: that in a modern business environment there simply is not the time or space for such luxuries, and that instead success requires some clear, decisive, distinctly unitarist leadership?

UNDER NEW MANAGEMENT

The starting point of the book is an examination of the big changes going on in the management of our organisations. Books about employee relations that start at the other end seem to me to miss the point. The institutions, procedures and practices of industrial or employee relations (I tend to use the terms interchangeably) are outcomes, not driving forces. They are shaped by the business forces that drive organisations and represent one of the significant ways in which organisations and those who work within them respond to those forces. Particularly over the hectic last 15 or so years, the dynamic for change in the management of people has come quite clearly from employers, and so it is with them that we begin.

In Chapter 2 the spotlight is on the new paradigm of management that has emerged for employers in response to pressures on traditional ways and which, in part at least, is shaping their behaviour as managers. The chapter charts the powerful forces that have been instrumental in reshaping the face of work. The increased competitiveness of world markets, the much sharper emphasis on the quality of output and the adoption of new, more flexible methods of production and service delivery, all these together with the thrust of government policy have wrought huge changes in the balance between sectors of the economy, employment patterns and skill profiles.

Behind the detail of these changes are the elements of the big picture: the 'D words' and the 'F words'. The D words – decentralisation, devolution, deregulation – describe the main ways in which organisations have reconfigured themselves to cope with the massive changes facing them. The F words – fast, flat and flexible – are about the organisational behaviour required for business success. Put them together and we have a model or paradigm for the successful, adaptive organisation. It is nimble, quick to react flexibly to external forces; it is outward looking and responsive, unencumbered by unnecessary organisational levels and bureaucratic procedures. Above all, it embraces a radically changed 'contract' with its employees. It emphasises the 'soft' elements of culture, style and values. It promotes organisational flatness and 'empowerment' rather than command, control and compliance. Managers become 'facilitators' and coaches. Horizontal processes and teams take over from vertical functions and organisation charts. That is the theory.

Certainly, the chapter points out, managers have been creating space for themselves within which to make such a shift. In particular they have been internalising their labour markets and employee relations structures, cutting links with external bodies and arrangements, and putting the spotlight on the pursuit of the specific needs of the business. But, as the chapter concludes, it would be wrong to take the image of the new paradigm at face value. The two missing dimensions are power, the recognition that there is still at heart an inequity in the balance of the employment relationship, and an account of what managers actually do with their new-found space for action.

Chapter 3 approaches these issues from a different but related angle. Here we try and get inside the head of the modern manager. How does he or she seek to make connections between, at one end the ever-changing configuration of competitive business pressures, and at the other end the pattern of employment and the practice of employee relations? To what extent can we produce a model or models that can help predict how managers will translate changes in external market conditions into employee relations outcomes?

There is no shortage of frameworks and theories in this area. There are models that analyse the main categories of strategic response to competitive pressures, that show how an organisation can choose its principal weapons: a focus on innovation, for example, or on cost reduction, or on quality. Equally there is a solid body of literature that explores the connections between business strategy and organisational structure on the one hand and management style on the other.

Chapter 3 shows that it is quite possible to establish business-based frameworks for connecting up corporate strategy in its widest sense with the principal features of employee relations. So, for example, we can set out the key employee relations features that are likely to result from, say, the pursuit of a competitive strategy based on high product quality in an organisation that manages its subsidiaries on a fairly loose rein. Conversely we can paint the likely employee relations picture of a cost-controlling organisation managed tightly according to bottom line results.

All such models, however, are analytical devices, showing what logically might be expected to happen given the presence or otherwise of particular circumstances. The missing ingredient is the one that brings it all to life: the mental map, the 'mindset', the received wisdom of the managers actually taking the decisions that will determine the strategic response to market conditions and then translate this response into organisational and employment reality.

The crucial model then is the one inside managers' heads – the one that encompasses key assumptions about how people are best managed, about what motivates them, about what constitutes fair and reasonable treatment.

This leads us straight from the rarefied atmosphere of strategy formulation to the more down to earth stuff of strategy implementation – to the practical business of making it all happen. Here we find an important tension. On the one hand is the rather 'top down', unitarist process of strategy formulation – at least as it is practised in most organisations. On the other hand is a body of research and experience covering the management of change that paints a much more pluralist picture. This tells us that change is managed best on the basis of involvement, participation and commitment. It argues for the empowerment of employees as the best route to securing lasting and profitable change. But it recognises that in most change processes, if employees are empowered, managers are even more empowered.

A crucial issue of trust therefore arises. Do managers trust their employees enough to let go: to truly empower them with the implementation of key aspects of corporate strategy? Do employees conversely trust their managers enough to give up the defensive, protective powers they might once have had to make themselves secure *against* change, and make the leap of commitment needed to seek security *in* change? The challenge for the new management then is to establish a framework that can help both managers and employees make this major shift.

That shift is the focus of Chapter 4. Have British managers adopted the banner of 'human resource management' (HRM) as the device for effecting this shift? At first sight HRM seems to offer the right sort of framework. It is based on a notion of 'integration' – that decisions about the employment and management of people should be firmly rooted in the business strategy of the organisation and should not have an independent life of their own. It is also highly focused on the relationship with and development of the *individual* employee, rather than on the collective regulation of relations with employees *en masse*. Key words in the HRM lexicon are 'flexibility', 'quality' and 'commitment': words at the heart of the strategic challenge facing business organisations.

Chapter 4 looks for the distinctive features of HRM and concludes that there are five. First, it is aimed firmly at the management and development of management teams. Second, it is inextricably bound up with the shifting of responsibility for staff management to line managers. Third, it relies heavily on the active management of organisational culture, as the 'glue' that replaces the more procedurally-based framework of traditional personnel management. Fourth, it is, in the fullest sense, about the more systematic *exploitation* of the labour force in pursuit of corporate goals. Fifth and above all, it represents a shift in the ownership of people-management issues from the 'experts' of personnel and industrial relations to the mainstream of the general management line. It is, in other words, about the discovery of personnel management by chief executives and general managers.

Looked at through the lens of employee relations, HRM is therefore a challenging force. It is challenging to unions because it is individualistic in focus and unitarist in tone and spirit. It is a model that seeks to 'fit' the human resource to the organisation's strategic purpose rather than seeking to reach an accommodation with it. (That said, one of the interesting findings of later chapters is that it is precisely in unionised environments that many of the key features of HRM can most commonly be found – Chapter 5 investigates the possible reasons for this.) Equally however the concepts of human resource management pose big challenges for managers. Do middle-level line managers have the competence to make constructive use of the tools that are to be put into their hands? Can they manage the more focused, individual relationships with their staff that emerge when the protective cover of personnel 'rules' is removed?

The evidence is that many are found wanting when faced with these challenges. The range and variety of different practices sailing under the HRM flag raise doubts about the usefulness of the device as a way of describing change. Certainly there are instances of quite fundamental reshaping of employee relations very much along the lines of the HRM model. At the other end of the spectrum there are plenty of cases of quite unreconstructed management practices being relabelled as human resource management. The intensification of effort extracted from workforces and the imposition of less secure and less rewarding working patterns in many parts of the labour market hardly squares with HRM's emphasis on commitment, development and shared values, and with the claim that people are 'our greatest asset'.

In the middle there is a more opportunistic mix. A bit more flexibility, a greater emphasis on staff development and 'competencies' and a lot more performance management: but does this add up to a whole new model for managing people, a genuine sense of 'under new management'?

However, in a narrower sense, the relationship between organisations and their employees clearly is under new management. As the initiative in the management of people has passed from the personnel and industrial relations community to general management so the agenda and definition of the area has changed. The agenda of 'people issues' of this community is different. It is concerned with issues of cost control, the 'fit' of individuals to new systems and structures, and skill mismatches. It has a 'project management' approach to the management of change – a sequencing of tasks, not a winning of hearts and minds; and it is instinctively unitarist, impatient with any institution or procedure that poses a barrier to change or that seeks to offer a competing outlook or represent a separate constituency.

NEW EMPLOYEE RELATIONS

So what has this new management set out to achieve in the field of employee relations? After 15 or more years of non-stop pressure on the established structures and institutions of industrial relations has the old mould been broken for good? If one model has been dismantled – with its unionised workforces, its emphasis on collective bargaining and on a jointly regulated 'rulebook' – has it been replaced systematically with another equally pervasive model? If not, then what is the spectrum of mainstream choice within which organisations are now refashioning their employee relations, and is there a trend in any particular direction?

These questions provide the focus for Chapters 5 and 6, with the case studies of Chapter 7 throwing in some additional practical pointers. The underlying issue is this: employers have been given an unprecedented amount of space within which to make untrammelled choices about the manner in which they are going to organise and conduct their relationships with their employees; how in practice are they using their new powers and freedoms?

The extent to which the employee relations rulebook has been rewritten is nothing short of revolutionary. The combined impact of 'step by step' legislation together with changes in management practice and workplace organisation has been to destroy the principal features of British industrial relations. These revolved around the concept of 'voluntarism'. This concept meant that the law would give sufficient 'immunities' to trade unions in order to let them operate legally within the law of contract, and then stand aside, holding the ring, while the institutions of industrial relations reached collective agreements, whose terms were then imported into individual enterprises.

In place of that tradition we now have a highly-prescriptive legal framework for the conduct of employee relations, which is based on what has been called the 'doctrine of enterprise confinement'. This means that:

- Employers have become more free to decide the basis on which they are to conduct their employee relations – whether with or without unions.
- They can largely inoculate themselves from agreements, rules and procedures, drawn up outside their gates.
- Trade unions, conversely, now have to operate within a regulatory environment that is arguably tighter than for any other group in society – certainly when compared to the self regulating set-ups of the financial services sector.
- In particular, trade unions have no legal scope to act on issues that fall outside the immediate 'bread and butter' concerns of the members' workplace.

Caught between the legislative squeeze on the one hand and the impact of economic restructuring on traditional areas of membership, trade unions have not surprisingly had a thin time of it. Membership is down one-third from its high point of 1979. The proportion of the workforce in unions is down from well over 50 per cent to around one-third, with a corresponding decline in the proportion of the working population covered by collective agreements. The remaining area of unionised employee relations has about it something of the appearance of an eroding island in a sea that is at best indifferent towards it, at worst downright hostile.

Chapter 8 looks at these developments from the viewpoint of the unions themselves. It is critical in its judgements. It paints a picture of organisations which – using a commercial analogy – have seen demand in their core markets plummet but which have done little to develop new products or open up new markets. Faced with the ever-growing trend towards the individualisation of employment relationships and management techniques, the unions have continued to plug away at selling collective bargaining to employers – and indeed to employees, to whom it is increasingly irrelevant.

They have certainly not measured up to the challenge to 're-engineer' themselves in the way that major industrial concerns have, when faced with a crisis of similar proportions. This means fundamentally reappraising what it is that customers and potential customers require, and then reshaping all processes and structures to deliver the required service at lowest cost and to highest standard.

EMPLOYER CHOICE IN PRACTICE

So, three powerful forces have come together to expand greatly the area of choice available to employers in their conduct of employee relations:

■ A legal framework that enables them to be masters in their own house to a degree that is virtually unprecedented this century, and without current parallel in other industrial countries.
■ A tremendous weakening of the sources of pluralist 'checks and balances' to employer power – notably the trade unions.
■ A wide adoption of the tools, techniques, and models of management that enable employers to use this new-found space in order to align the way in which they manage their people with the requirements of their business strategy.

After a decade and more of such new freedom of choice, and with an entire economic cycle on which to reflect, it is timely to try and draw up the balance sheet. How, in practice, have employers used their new powers and freedoms? Have they used them in ways that would support the creation of the high value 'people centred' paradigm of a successful organisation of the future? Have they behaved in ways that will get better performance out of employees now and a strengthening of their skills for the future? Is the net effect a positive one for the national economy and for the employees themselves?

Chapter 6 draws a map of the new mainstream of employer choice.

■ At one end of the spectrum is the small number of organisations who seek actively to involve their employees' trade unions as partners in their plans.
■ Next comes the large swathe of organisations in which the structures and processes of industrial relations survive but are the subject of massive managerial indifference.
■ Shading into this segment is another one in which these same structures are maintained but are subjected not to indifference, but to sustained and visible hostility.
■ Next comes the straightforwardly-unitarist segment in which either an employer has derecognised trade unions (an increasingly common feature, as the chapter spells out) or has set up a new operation on a non-union, usually individualistic basis.
■ Finally there is the long tail of the non-union private sector,

accounting for half or more of the employed workforce and embracing some distinctly backward practices: reduced levels of health and safety at work, higher labour turnover and more employment insecurity, lower pay, lower morale, poorer communications.

Four conclusions stand out from this analysis. First, it is the latter two sectors that are growing, in relative and absolute terms. The motor force for redrawing the employee relations map is therefore a set of organisations whose approach to the management of people is clearly unitarist, intolerant of what they would see as 'interference' from such outsiders as trade unions, but tolerant of employment conditions which have in the past acted as recruiting agents for trade unionism.

Second, there is scope for the application of the techniques and indeed of the framework of human resource management across this spectrum. We might expect to find it most readily in the growing, unitarist-inclined sectors described above. It is a fact, however that the adoption of the key practices of HRM has been most common in the unionised sector – partly no doubt as part of employer strategies to weaken the link between unions and their members.

Third, it is clear from this that in many significant organisations there is a substantial gap between the way in which people are managed and the management of the rest of the enterprise. Institutions and practices from a pluralist past that is no longer valued are maintained out of indifference, inertia or a desire to let sleeping dogs lie, but nothing positive is then done with or through them. The structures through which the relationship between employer and employee is formally conducted are the subject of managerial disinterest and no attempt is made to connect them up to the dynamic processes in the organisation through which change is conceived and implemented. In the literature this is called 'industrial relations dualism'. 'Wasted opportunity' is a phrase that springs more readily to mind.

The final conclusion is that for many individual employees the net effect of all these changes has been a pretty bleak one – certainly one that is a long way removed from the picture of them as 'most highly valued assets' painted in the more exuberant management texts. Viewed from their perspective, what we see in the changes of the last decade and a half is the removal, piece by piece, of the safety nets, minimum standards and floors that limited the downside risk from the changes to which they were exposed. We hear much of the greater energy and dynamism that has been released into the economy through this process, and about the winners from it. We would also do well to remember that it has been a process from which there have been very many losers.

WHAT PRICE THE NEW WORLD OF WORK?

The balance sheet of change then is a mixed one. Many have been bruised by the process. Equally, for many the experience has been a positive one, enabling them either as employers or employees to do things from which they were previously prohibited or inhibited. For many organisations, including some of the case study organisations covered in Chapter 7, the changes have been liberating and empowering.

What we do not have from this account is a picture of one, all-embracing new 'system' of employee relations replacing its predecessor. The picture is one that is much more akin to a kaleidoscope or a patchwork quilt. But then that is the whole point about an approach to employee relations based on employer choice!

If this means that it is difficult to generalise about the experience of individual organisations and employees in the new world of work, we can still try and draw out the wider implications for the economy. If there have been economic gains, in terms of greater flexibility, better cost control and so on, what price has been paid along the way. What are the macro costs from the reshaping of employee relations? What might be the benefits of reinstating some of the lost pluralism – the elements of challenge, of recognition of different interests and constituencies, of seeking compromise and consensus – into the new pattern of employee relations?

The case for a greater degree of pluralism is threefold. First, there is the recognition that it can be the best vehicle for addressing economic 'externalities': the features that all organisations need in order to be effective, but which will not be in the interest of individual organisations to invest. Things like the creation of standards for safe and healthy working conditions, of skills that are transferable between organisations, of non-discriminatory working practices: these add to the ability of all organisations to operate effectively, but will often be on or beyond the margins of concern for an inwardly-focused unitarist body. Pluralist structures and processes, industry level arrangements, negotiated codes of conduct, sector-wide agreements – all of which can seem tiresome and irrelevant to a performance-driven enterprise – can therefore add a source of strength to the new world of work.

Second, there is an argument for pluralism that centres on the dynamics of change and which relates to the concepts of *trust* and *consent*. Pluralism, especially in the form of independent employee representation, offers the workforce a *voice*, and this does two things. It provides managers with a source of information about workplace issues and concerns that they might otherwise not have, and it provides the workforce with a degree of confidence that their worries and concerns will be heard and indeed acted upon. This in turn gives them the extra bit of confidence to 'let go' and to participate more positively in new and changed ways of working.

The extra element of trust that is injected in this way is of particular importance at a time when new technologies and management practices – such as just-in-time production, teamworking and de-layering – give both managers and workforce a significantly greater degree of potential power over the other. Only by building a greater element of trust, runs the argument, can organisations ensure that this potential power is not used in a negative way (against one another) but that, instead, it is turned outward into competitive advantage. And that trust will only be forthcoming if each of the parties feels that if things were ever to come to the crunch they would have a clear right to say 'no'.

The third argument for an extra degree of pluralism is the most straightforward one. In a period of greater deregulation, when previous protections have been removed and some highly-questionable employment practices have emerged, simple fairness demands that employees have someone on their side, to look after their interests. And it is not enough to say that the someone in question should be the employer who, using new powers and freedoms, has created the conditions that now demand redress. The case for pluralism in the economic sphere, in other words, is the same as the case for it in the political sphere: as a set of checks and balances against the abuse of executive power.

The problem is, as Chapter 9 points out, that however persuasive a case this is on paper, in the workplace it is cutting little, if any, ice. In many organisations the management community simply cannot conceive of there being a positive case for, in their terms, giving up power and influence and sharing it with bodies which do not see their prime loyalty as being to the policy of the organisation, as articulated by the management. They can see no immediate benefit for themselves in taking a more pluralistic approach and they are quite impervious to suggestions that they should have a wider view towards the interests of the economy beyond the confines of their own firm. And of course in an era in which employee relations is constructed on the basis of their own preferences and choices, such attitudes are decisive.

This coin has another side, however. A pattern of employee relations that tilts the balance of influence so firmly towards managers, by the same token raises the ante on their ability to discharge successfully their newly-expanded role. In other words the spotlight now shines brightly on the competence of managers to build trust, manage performance and generally get the best out of their people, with fewer visible means of support.

It is one of the ironies of this area that the more rigid, rule-bound and restrictive employee relations framework of the past suited well the purposes and temperament of a certain type of manager. For them the business of managing people was always (and still remains) very difficult indeed. The old system may have erected many barriers, but some of those barriers were also shields – removing the responsibility of having to engage in the troublesome business of actually managing their staff directly, and simul-taneously providing a set of handy scapegoats – the unions, Per-sonnel – for when things went wrong.

Remove the shield, and managers have to manage the relation-ship with their employees directly and in the full glare of light created by their bold statements about the responsibility that they are now taking on for aligning the management of their people with the business goals of the organisation as a whole. And there is plenty of evidence that the level of managerial competence, in many organisations, and indeed sectors, is not up to this challenge.

Whether measured in the under-performance of workforces, in the inattention to their training and development, in the level of dissatisfaction routinely expressed by employees on the receiving end of the new employee relations, or in the levels of stress experienced by middle managers with the responsibility for managing people thrust upon them, but without the support they feel necessary to fulfil this responsibility, the conclusion is the same: we are not making the best of the opportunities we now have.

We have lost many of the advantages of the old, more pluralist approach. At the same time our ability to get more out of the new pattern of employee relations is constrained by the level of man-agerial competence in something which the UK, by dint of its history, education, class system and structures, has always done badly – the effective, productive and humane management of large numbers of people.

This underlines the need for two things. The first is a general raising of the ability of UK managers to manage people. The level of managerial skill is a crucial determinant of the ability of a system – based on employer choice – to operate effectively. The second, and perhaps more paradoxical, is for the trade unions to do more to get their act together. For only they can persuasively make the case for injecting a stronger dose of pluralism into the realm of employee relations. Without a strong and effective push from them we seem set to continue to under-perform. If they can discover the grain of the new employee relations and work with it, they can, perhaps, re-establish themselves in the position that they best occupy: that of a hinge between employers and employees – understanding the interests of each and helping each achieve more than they would be capable of alone.

CHAPTER 2

The Changing Face of Work

INTRODUCTION

The last decade and a half has witnessed accelerating pressure on organisations to change. Some of the pressures for change have been new. Many were in evidence before the 1980s but have been given a new urgency in the 1980s and 1990s. Some of the pressures have been common across the industrialised world; others still have had a distinctly 'made in the UK' flavour to them.

Taken together these pressures have brought about a dramatic transformation in the economic and industrial landscape, reshaping many patterns and features that had previously been taken for granted as distinct and lasting aspects of the economic scene. Some of these changes have been visible – and widely discussed – at national level. The decline of UK manufacturing industry and the growing importance of inward investment as a source of employment, the growth, in the 1980s at least, of service sector activity, are all examples of widely recognised phenomena.

Many of these changes have also, however, had a profound, if less visible, impact below the surface of organisations: on the pattern and nature of the work that is carried out within them. Indeed, many of the changes of the last decade or so have in subtle ways reshaped the way in which we think about the world of work – its availability, its place in our lives, and the relationships that go with it. In short, there have been significant shifts in the way in which work is organised and structured for many groups of employees, and this has been accompanied by some significant changes in the values and attitudes attached to the world of work.

This chapter is designed to take us through the significant changes, starting with the macro and going through to the micro, or local. The starting point is a brief account of some of the most striking features of the changed landscape of recent years. We look at various measures of change in the structure of economic activity, at the pattern of trade, at changes in the pattern of ownership of organisations. We also examine the changing structure of employment and of occupations in the UK. This reminder of the changing scene is followed by an analysis of the major business pressures that have been instrumental in producing this pattern of changes in the economy.

We then summarise the way in which these pressures have manifested themselves within organisations. Many of the familiar D words stand out – decentralisation, deregulation, divisionalisation, devolution – and with them we find some important shifts in the imagery and values attached to organisations as providers of work, and indeed to work itself. This is the context within which we first encounter the phrase 'human resource management' – which will figure so prominently in later parts of this book. We take a first brief look at the significance of this term as part of the new way of looking at work. The chapter ends, however, with a reminder of the need to keep a sense of proportion: within a landscape that has changed considerably there remain many important features of continuity in which more traditional aspects, attitudes and values are exhibited.

THE CHANGING LANDSCAPE

Changes in the structure of the UK economy have been widespread and complex and have accelerated markedly in the 1980s and 1990s. Picking our way through the data and trends we come across some strong new patterns that help to define the shape and texture of economic activity in the UK today – and some of the important ways in which that pattern stands out from movements elsewhere in Europe. Among the most prominent features are the following:

- The shift away from manufacturing activity and towards the services sector, whether measured in terms of share of GDP, employment or investment.
- The decline in 'traditional' full-time employment and the rise in part-time and 'non-standard' forms of employment (temporary, contract, self-employed, etc).
- The growth in female, and decline in male, employment.
- The movement of economic activity away from the traditional industrial areas and large cities and towards the 'cathedral

cities', suburbs and the south (notwithstanding the rapid rise in unemployment in these latter areas in the early 1990s).

■ The reduction in the relative size of the public sector – partly through privatisation, partly through continuous squeezing of the resources available to all activities remaining in the public sector.

■ Massive restructuring of commercial enterprises characterised, among other things, by widespread changes in – and continuing concentration of – ownership of companies, accompanied by a reduction in the average size of operating units. The decline in the large workplace – the home of the British industrial relations system – is a prominent feature of this period.

Many attempts have been made to capture the essence of these changes in a memorable phrase: 'deindustrialisation', 'post-Fordism', 'from sunset to sunrise industries', and so on. Certainly for our purposes it is important to note the relative and absolute decline of a form of economic activity which has long held a central place in our image of industry and work – in broad terms the male manual worker employed in a large manufacturing workplace north of Watford – and the rise of new paradigms: notably that of the female employee working other than on a full time basis in a smallish service organisation in the suburbs. As we shall see later, one further noteworthy point is that the former image relates very closely to a widely held stereotype of the 'typical' trade union member, while the latter group have traditionally found themselves outside trade union membership, not least because of the tendency of many trade unions to regard them as somehow not doing 'proper' jobs.

Many forces have combined to create the pattern of change charted here. Macroeconomic forces have played a large part. The policy regime of the 1980s substantially tightened the exchange rate pressure on the UK's trading sector and gave a severe twist to the decline of manufacturing. Financial services deregulation both changed the pattern of demand by prompting the debt-financed boom of the late 1980s, and gave a major boost to the size of the financial services sector itself. And of course the recession of the 1990s has in turn taken some of the air out of the financial services bubble, but has also produced a further decline in the manu-facturing sector to the point where, at the time of writing, total manufacturing employment exceeds the number of unemployed in the country by fewer than one million.

If we go below the macro level, however, and look at the turbulence of the last decade and a half from the viewpoint of the firm, we would describe the forces driving for change in the following terms.

THE DRIVERS FOR CHANGE

Among the plethora of pressures bearing in on firms, the following stand out:

■ Increasing competitiveness in international markets which has put ever-stronger cost pressure on UK firms. During the 1980s the proportion of UK GDP that was traded internationally grew significantly: exports up from 42 to 46 per cent, imports from 43 to 51 per cent. This was also the decade which opened with the rapid growth of the newly industrialised and fiercely competitive economies of the Pacific rim and closed with the sudden opening up in the, hitherto largely closed, markets of eastern Europe.

■ The growing importance of quality of production and of service delivery as decisive competitive differentiators in all markets with, as we shall see below, decisive consequences for production methods, organisational structures and working patterns. The increasingly central position of quality was captured in a report from the MIT Commission on Industrial Productivity. 'Partly because of internationalisation and partly because of rising income levels around the world, markets for consumer goods and intermediate goods are becoming more sophisticated. In many countries, consumers and commercial buyers are becoming more knowledgable and more quality-conscious. Markets are also becoming more segmented and specialised; not everyone is prepared to accept the same designs and specifications. As this process continues, consumers will expect products progressively more customised to individual taste.'[1]

■ The growing importance – aided by the explosive growth in computer-based technologies – of flexible methods of production and of customer service delivery. Increasingly the emphasis has been on short-run, batch production, on reduced set-up and turn round times, on cutting the product development cycle and thus the time taken to bring new products and services to market. Much attention has been focused as a result on a series of new techniques, many of them Japanese-inspired, such as just-in-time production and materials requirements planning, as well as on the drive, described below, for 'total quality'.

THE RESPONSE

Just as these drivers have manifested themselves in different ways in different sectors and for different organisations, so too the way in which organisations have responded has varied enormously. Some common threads are visible however: a series of reactions revolving around what we might call the D-words.

1. *Diversification.* Faced with increasing competition, technological change and significant changes in demand patterns, a common strategic response has been to spread risk and seek competitive advantages through diversifying the product range and the portfolio of businesses controlled, frequently through takeover. This development has built upon a trend which is visible over a longer timescale. Thus, for example, between 1960 and 1980, of the top 200 UK enterprises, the proportion that could be classified as single businesses (ie deriving not less than 95 per cent of sales from one basic business) fell by more than half – from 22 per cent to just under 10 per cent. Conversely, the proportion falling into the category of 'related businesses' (where sales are distributed among a series of related businesses such that no one accounts for 70 per cent of sales) grew from 33 to 50 per cent.[2]

2. *Decentralisation.* The pressure to be more responsive to a more rapidly changing competitive environment, to be flexible, nimble and fleet of foot has led organisations to decentralise activities wherever possible and to turn away from large scale, centralised, head-office type functions. The objective is to separate strategic from operational concerns and management – keeping a tight grip over the former while allowing local managers the freedom to implement the strategy.

3. *Devolution.* The counterpart to decentralisation has been the move to devolve profit responsibility to ever-lower levels within the subsidiary, strategic business unit or operating unit. The clear profit responsibility that is defined in this way lies at the heart of the tight part of the system, of which the relatively greater freedom and flexibility on the operational side is the loose part.

4. *Deregulation.* Much of what we have been describing relates

very strongly to the private sector, where the exposure to external competitive pressures has taken place. A distinctive feature of the UK's experience since 1979, however, is that the deliberate policy of the government has been to create, wherever possible within the public sector, facsimiles of the same forces that have reshaped the private sector. At one extreme of course we have seen privatisation, which has simply taken a large slice of economic activity out of the public sector into the fully trading private sector where, to the extent that the enterprises concerned have not been protected by monopoly status, they have been exposed to the same pressures as the rest of the commercial sector. For the rest of the public sector these forces have been emulated by a combination of:

— Creation of internal markets, as in the health service through the separation of roles between purchaser and service provider.
— Delegation of budgetary responsibility through programmes such as the Financial Management Initiative.
— Separation of strategic and operational management, most noticeably through the next steps programme which puts all but a radically slimmed-down 'core' of policymakers into arm's length bodies with their own business plans, 'product' focus and 'profit targets'.
— Contracting out of many activities through compulsory competitive tendering in local authority services and 'market testing' in central government.
— An emphasis on quality through the Citizen's Charter concept of establishing published, monitored standards of service provision.

THE DRIVE FOR QUALITY

This picture of the pressures for change on UK businesses, and of their response to those pressures, would be incomplete, however, without including two major ingredients. The first is the concept of total quality management (TQM) which spread rapidly in the 1980s in response to the growing recognition of the pressure, described above, to compete increasingly on grounds of quality, and in response, too, to a widespread sentiment that there were important lessons to be learned from Japanese businesses about making the management of quality integral to all operations. The TQM concept rests on the following core principles:

- A 'customer first' orientation – to internal and external customers alike.
- A commitment, from the top of the organisation to all levels, to the goal of continuous improvement.
- A stress on 'designing quality in' before production rather than on trying to 'inspect it in' afterwards.
- The use of the concept of 'cost of quality' and of statistical process measurement to reduce variation and wastage.
- Recognition of, and respect for, the contribution of the workforce to the improvement of quality, and a willingness to change the culture of the organisation to allow for this contribution to be made.

In terms of the way in which we look at the world of work the widespread (but by no means universal) adoption of parts of the total quality canon has had a number of significant consequences, among which the following ones stand out:

- *The inversion of the organisation chart.* Total quality thinking encourages firms to turn the chart upside down. Instead of starting with the elevated chief executive and then working down through successive layers of hierarchy to the lowly level of operative, the starting point is the customer and the front-line workers who are in direct contact with them. The other levels of the structure are then defined in terms of the support that they provide to that critical point of interaction.
- *'Delayering' the organisation.* By removing unnecessary reporting levels a better focus is achieved on the point of contact with customers. The model here is of the 'flatter' organisation within which there are fewer blockages to the transmission of information, and a greater emphasis on teamworking and cross-functional operations, in contrast to the traditional model of functional compartments.
- *From supervision to 'empowerment'.* TQM embraces a fundamental shift in the way in which we look at the management of the production worker. The logical consequence of the century-long reliance on the 'scientific management' school (embodied most notably in the work of Frederick Taylor) had been the ever-finer division of labour, the consequent de-skilling of production employees and the replacement of their craft-based judgement with increasingly more sophisticated (and oppressive) systems of production control. This was the era of the supervisor as policeman, and of an approach to quality that was

based on 'inspecting it in' after an essentially 'irresponsible' workforce had done their worst.

Total quality thinking purports to stand the traditional approach on its head by emphasising that the solution to a production problem is more likely to reside in the head of the operative than of the manager, that quality has to be 'built in' rather than 'inspected in', and therefore that a workforce that is given genuinely-delegated responsibility for aspects of production, and is 'empowered' to discharge that responsibility, will achieve superior levels of performance to a workforce that is expected to conform to rules handed down from above, and whose conformance is ensured through successive layers of supervisory management.

THE SEARCH FOR FLEXIBILITY

The second outstanding ingredient affecting the way in which we look at the world of work is the concept of 'flexibility'. Already we have seen the growing importance assigned to flexible methods of production as part of the response to the intensification of competitive pressures. Going beyond this, however, the mid-1980s saw an increasing preoccupation with the need to apply the concept of flexibility to the organisation and conduct of all aspects of work.

In part this was driven by the economic views of government ministers and advisors who held that the key difference between dynamic economies and their more 'sclerotic' European counterparts lay in the additional degree of labour market flexibility enjoyed by the former. The way to create more jobs, on this account, therefore was to 'free up' the labour market by removing rules and regulations governing the terms and conditions on which labour could be employed, and weaken the institutions (notably trade unions, but also bodies such as wages councils) which stood in the way of the employer's untrammelled flexibility over the terms on which labour was employed.

Running alongside this development was the emergence of a rather different account of 'flexibility', which had its origins in an attempt to understand and classify what employers were already trying to do rather than in exhortations on them to behave differently. The key observation concerned the evidence of a growing segmentation in the labour market which was influentially described by John Atkinson and his colleagues at the Institute for Manpower Studies in terms of an apparent attempt by employers to differentiate between a 'core' and a 'peripheral' workforce.[3]

In this model the core group consists of skilled workers, managers and specialists for whom the firm has a continuing need. Flexibility in this core group is pursued by means of what is termed 'functional flexibility'. The key features of this strategy, according to Atkinson, include multi-skilling and multi-role working to enhance the mobility of this valued asset, more team working and a general increase in levels of training. In return this core group are offered better wages, job security, and most of the non-wage conditions of employment traditionally reserved for white-collar staff.

Clustered around this core group are three other groups of workers who together make up the periphery and whose employment, argues Atkinson, is characterised by 'numerical flexibility'.This periphery is described as, in effect, a series of buffers that enable the employer to vary the size and composition of the labour force in response to market conditions, and to do so in such a way as to protect to the greatest degree possible the position of the core. There are the less skilled, more routine workers who usually work full-time but without the job security or advantageous conditions enjoyed by the core. They are likely to have their overtime or shift patterns varied at short notice if production turns down. Then there are the part-time and temporary workers who experience even less advantageous conditions and employment protection and stand to have their contractual hours cut or even removed altogether. Beyond them lie the first buffer group: those whose employment relationship with the firm has been contracted out or out-sourced.

At the time of its publication, the IMS model gained a considerable amount of publicity and appeared to be a neat way of encapsulating some important apparent trends in the organisation of work in response to more turbulent and demanding product markets. It was not, however received without controversy. It appeared to hover unsteadily between being an empirical description of what employers were actually doing, a conceptual device to classify what they might do in response to external pressures and a policy prescription, advising them how they should respond. (Although Atkinson himself generally took the line that it fell firmly into the second of these categories.) As a result, however, the model attracted criticisms on all three grounds.

■ In empirical terms, Incomes Data Services concluded its 1986 study by saying that 'with very few exceptions ... one can say that the process of achieving full-scale flexibility has hardly begun'. Two years later they commented that 'the overall picture remains extremely uneven'. Anna Pollert concluded her study of changes in employment patterns in ringing terms: 'the "flexible firm" model is left standing with few clothes ... with little evidence of polarisation between an ill-defined "periphery" and a privileged "core" '.[4]

■ In conceptual terms the model was criticised for misrepresenting the way in which employers were likely to respond to product market turbulence. Historically, it was argued, UK firms had been as quick to lay off skilled workers as unskilled in a recession. And did not the persistence of skill shortages and of comparatively low levels of investment in training speak eloquently about the likelihood of the leopard of the British employer changing its spots?

■ Finally, in policy terms, the model was accused of providing respectable cover for the pursuit of some pretty disreputable practices. Was it not significant that the peripheral workforce appeared to be overwhelmingly female? Was not the model therefore simply inviting employers to give a further twist to an ingrained habit of segmenting the labour market in ways that systematically discriminated against women? And was not the apparent promotion of 'two tier' employment part and parcel of a general and undesirable polarisation in society between haves and have nots?

And yet ... It is a striking fact that despite some well- and fiercely-argued attacks on the model of the flexible firm and of flexible employment, the concept has proved markedly resilient: it has staying power. The language and imagery of the flexible firm seems to have passed into the management lexicon of the 1990s, where it has taken its place alongside concepts such as 'delayering', 'customer orientation' and 'culture change'. To take just one example, the procedure prescribed for government departments to follow when undertaking 'market testing' – the process through which government activities are made to compete with external contractors – speaks of the need to separate out 'core' from 'non-core' functions and jobs.

Why should this be? In part it might be that the empirical, conceptual and policy strands have, to some extent, come together in a mutually reinforcing synthesis. Organisations may, at the margin, have adjusted their employment practices in order to join what the conference circuit would have told them was fast becoming mainstream behaviour, thereby helping to bring the model to life. Similarly, aspects of the government's labour market policy – the reduction in the powers and coverage of the Wages Councils in the 1986 Wages Act and the successive measures to reduce the employment protection available to part-time, temporary and female workers are examples that come to mind – may have been justified in terms of 'cutting with the grain' of the supposedly more flexible practices of firms, but were in reality designed to bring these practices into being.

This does not seem, however, to be a sufficiently strong explanation. Instead it seems more likely that the lasting resonance of the concept of employment flexibility stems from the fact that it chimes strongly with some powerful, wider imagery which includes the concept of flexibility but which takes it further into areas which have even more profound implications for the way in which we think about, and structure, the world of work. It is to that body of thought that we must now turn.

FAST, FLAT, FLEXIBLE AND FUNKY

It is a virtual certainty that anyone who has come into a management position, whether in the private or the public sector, in manufacturing, financial services or retail, will have been exposed to a set of concepts and images (and indeed normative values) which are characterised by the heading of this section. The contact may only have been fleeting but the roll of honour will include names that at the very least will ring bells from a management development course dimly recalled or a conversation with a colleague who went off to do an MBA: Peters and Waterman, Rosabeth Moss Kanter, Charles Handy, Richard Pascale ... and so on. We have seen, in effect, the creation of a very powerful and persuasively argued paradigm of what a successful organisation looks like and, through this, of the likely future pattern of work. And this has been developed at a time of unprecedented restructuring and reorientation that has made businesses anxious for the comfort of a new model, and managers, at all levels, anxious to incorporate the new way of looking at the world into their managerial activities.

Let us summarise the main features of the new paradigm and draw out the major implications for the world of work. Here, to start us off, is Charles Handy[5] pushing the flexibility theme as far as he can make it go.

> The world of work is changing because the organisations of work are changing their ways. At the same time, however, the organisations are having to adapt to a changing world of work. It's a chicken and egg situation ... Instead of one workforce there are now three, (the core, the contactual fringe and the flexible labour force), each with a different kind of commitment to the organisation, a different contractual arrangement, a different set of expectations. They each have to be managed in different ways ... Organisations used to be perceived as gigantic pieces of engineering, with largely interchangeable human parts. We talked of their structures and their systems, of inputs and outputs, of control devices and of managing them, as if the whole was one large factory. Today the language is not that of engineering but of politics, with talk of cultures and networks, of teams and coalitions, of influence or power rather than control, of leadership not management.

With this account comes also Handy's concept of the 'inside-out do'nut' or 'fried egg' approach to job design and definition in which: 'The things you must do or you have failed, represent the solid core of the inside-out do'nut, the yolk of the egg ... More is expected. You are meant to fill up the whole of the do'nut, the white of the egg as well as the yolk.'[6]

At the heart of Charles Handy's image of the new-style organisation is the concept of 'Federalism' which he describes thus:[7]

> Federalism implies a variety of individual groups allied together under a common flag with some shared identity. Federalism seeks to make it big by keeping it small, or at least independent, by combining autonomy with cooperation. It is the method which businesses are slowly, and painfully, evolving for getting the best of both worlds – the size which gives them clout in the market-place and in the financial centres, as well as some economies of scale, and the small unit size which gives them the flexibility which they need, as well as the sense of community for which individuals increasingly hanker.

This account embraces a critique of organisational forms and work organisation in more traditional, Western businesses which was expressed at its most forceful by Tom Peters in *Thriving on Chaos*:[8] 'Decentralisation was the right strategy – it still is. But the "clean", business-minded structures envisioned by the pioneers lost their zip over time, and success didn't help. Many decentralised units grew big, with some divisions encumbered by ten or more layers of management.'

Tom Peters' response to all of this is to insist on three basic principles:

- Breaking organisations into the smallest possible 'independent' units.
- Giving every employee a businessperson's strong sense of revenue, cost and profit.
- Ever-closer involvement with the customer.

Organisational 'flatness' is a key part of the prescription. Peters says:[9]

> I insist on five management layers as the maximum. Incidentally, that's the number of layers with which the Catholic Church makes do to oversee 800 million members ... In fact, even the five-layer limit should apply only to very complex organisations such as multi-division firms. Three layers – supervisor (with the job redefined to deal with a span of control no smaller than one supervisor for twenty-five to seventy-five people), department head, and unit boss – should be tops for any single facility, such as a plant or operations or distribution center.

Against that background it is no surprise to find Peters, in his latest book, singing the praises of electrical power and equipment manufacturer Asea Brown Boveri, which employs 215,000 people in 5000 autonomous profit centres. Each profit centre has its own profit and loss account and balance sheet, each owns assets, and each serves customers directly. And taking the whole company there are only three layers of management from top to bottom.[10]

So, organisational flatness, the ability to react nimbly to radically-changing circumstances, the need, in Richard Pascale's words 'to live out of balance',[11] these are all core features of the new organisational and managerial paradigm of the 1990s: the vision of an excellent enterprise and the imagery taken into businesses of all types by aspiring managers.

Tom Peters has hardly been without his critics. His methodology has been questioned; his disregard of structure and systems has been criticised; and it has been pointed out that a large proportion of the companies originally identified by him and Waterman as being 'excellent' were in serious trouble ten years on. In a way, however, this is beside the point. What is significant is the power of the new paradigm and the extent to which it has become part of the customary language and imagery of managers in ever-larger numbers.

Pascale has captured the essence of the new paradigm in the following terms:[12]

■ *From* the image of organisations as machines, with the emphasis on concrete strategy, structure and systems, *to* the idea of organisations as organisms, with the emphasis on the 'soft' dimensions – style, staff, and shared values.

■ *From* a hierarchical model, with step-by-step problem solving, *to* a network model, with parallel nodes of intelligence which surround problems until they are eliminated.

■ *From* the status-driven view that managers think and workers do as they are told, *to* a view of managers as 'facilitators', with workers empowered to initiate improvements and change.

■ *From* an emphasis on 'vertical tasks' within functional units *to* an emphasis on 'horizontal tasks' and collaboration across units.

■ *From* a focus on 'content' and the prescribed use of specific tools and techniques *to* a focus on 'process' and a holistic synthesis of techniques.

■ *From* the military model *to* a commitment model.

Pulling these threads together, Pascale writes of this new 'mind-set':[13]

> While no individual trend is earthshaking, the aggregate impact of the whole cluster imposes more of a burden than our traditional approach to management can bear. The old focuses on managerial 'hardware' (specific techniques and financial objectives); the new encompasses 'software' (restlessness and creative tension). It is not that the 'hardware' is unimportant, but that it is insufficient.

Rosabeth Moss Kanter uses a different metaphor to come at what is essentially the same paradigm. In *The Change Masters*[14] she speaks of the magician's 'magic rings' which, tossed in the air, magically lock and unlock themselves:

> For a large part of its ongoing operations, an innovating organi- sation may look on the surface just like a segmented one. It has a clear structure; its organisation charts may show a differentiation into departments or functional units, there may be stated reporting relationships, and people may occupy specific jobs with specific job

descriptions and bounded responsibilities. Just like the magic rings, the parts can be separated and, for routine purposes, dealt with separately. But with the toss of a problem, the additional connections between and across segments become clear: executive teams considering problems together; crosscutting task forces; teams of employees pulling together to improve performance; networks of peers who exchange information and support each other's projects.

HERE COMES 'HUMAN RESOURCE MANAGEMENT'

We can summarise the bundle of pressures that are bearing down on organisations and reshaping the organisation of work and the relationship between the organisation and those who work within it.

We have seen the intensification of competition in product markets and the consequent pressure on firms to decentralise, to become more focused and, in particular, to put a far greater emphasis on quality, on customer service and on flexibility. Along with that – and partly in response to it – we have seen the passionate critique of bureaucratic and hierarchical organisational structures and processes and the advocacy of an alternative model that is much flatter and 'networked'. At the centre of this paradigm is a radically increased emphasis on a set of 'softer' processes and, indeed, values. Communication, autonomy, trust, respect, learning, and leadership (rather than management) emerge as critical components of this new bundle.

It is in this setting that we first encounter the term 'human resource management'. In Chapter 4 we will take a detailed look at what, both in principle and in practice, the phrase represents. For present purposes, however, a brief thumbnail sketch will serve. Human resource management (HRM) covers the ground which we traditionally associate with personnel management and with industrial relations, (although as we shall see later there is a problem here). It purports, however, to go further and to cover issues and areas which are of strategic importance to the organisation. It emerges from our consideration of the new management paradigm in part because its origins lie in the same American debates as the other aspects of the 'new thinking'.

More importantly, however, it arises here because of the agenda that it covers and the focus that it brings to bear on 'people issues'. The biggest shots in the HRM locker are:

- *Performance.* An emphasis on processes and systems that promote, measure and manage the performance of the workforce.
- *Development.* HRM espouses the need not just to maximise short term performance but also to develop the longer-run potential of the workforce – investing in human as well as physical capital, and in particular seeking to develop the capacity and skills of managers.
- *Culture.* A distinguishing feature of HRM is that it sees the culture of the organisation as something that can be shaped, adapted and managed. This is of crucial importance because, in making the shift away from military-style, command and control methods of management, organisations have a great need to use culture and values to reinforce behaviour and thus achieve the required control over performance.
- *Integration.* One of the hallmarks of HRM is that it seeks to bring together the otherwise disparate aspects of employment policy into a consistent whole – one, moreover, that supports the organisation's business strategy and which maximises the sense of commitment that the individual employee feels towards the organisation.

INTERNALISING THE EMPLOYMENT RELATIONSHIP

Not surprisingly, in view of this set of attributes, HRM has had a powerful appeal to organisations facing the kind of competitive pressures described in the earlier sections of this chapter. In particular it holds out the very attractive prospect of enabling the organisation to write its own rulebook for the way it manages its relationship with its employees: rules designed for its specific circumstances, culture and business objectives – indeed, individual rulebooks for individual business units within the organisation.

This sense of tailoring employment policy to business needs, of ceasing to 'import' rules, models and conditions from outside and switching instead to a more 'home grown' approach to the management of the employment relationship is a further defining feature of the bundle of changes described above. It belongs together with – and indeed is in many ways the logical corollary of – the competitive pressure to decentralise, to focus and to devolve.

This thinking has had a profound impact on the role and operations of the personnel function in many organisations. Traditionally the central holder of the rulebook, the function with the power to tell line managers what they could – and more typically what they could not – get away with in their dealings with their staff, personnel has been through its own decentralising revolution. The new paradigm that has emerged is of a small strategic resource at the centre of the organisation, designing policies and giving strategic advice, with day to day responsibility for managing people pushed down the line management chain.

In this way the employment relationship has been decentralised and indeed internalised to business units. This process ran into conflict with the essentially centralising and externally focused nature of much of the traditional industrial relations system in the UK. Not surprisingly, therefore, the decentralisation of personnel management responsibility has been accompanied by the withdrawal of organisations from industry-wide, multi-employer industrial relations arrangements in both public and private sectors.

Throughout this century this network of national agreements was the pre-eminent feature of the British employment scene. It was a system that suited employers because it limited the degree of competition between them over wages and conditions, and also tended to push the focus of trade union activity away from the workplace, where it might seem intrusive to employers, towards the national bargaining level where it could be dealt with at one remove by employers' associations. The system also happened to suit the business needs of trade unions because it produced a system of representation and negotiation that was relatively easy and cheap to service and maintain, not least because it was heavily subsidised by employers!

The effective coverage of this system was always much wider than the number of workers belonging to the unions who negotiated the national agreements, and therefore the majority of UK employers imported basic wage levels, non-wage conditions, skill categories and job definitions, together with working rules and procedural agreements governing the conduct of the employer/employee relationship.

Multi-employer arrangements have actually been on the decline for some time. The increasingly complex structure of British business, and in particular the rise of the divisionalised and conglomerate enterprise, has meant that an increasing number of firms simply have not fitted into the straightforward industrial categories of national bargaining. More pressingly, however, the need to respond more effectively to competitive pressures has sharply increased the number of organisations no longer prepared to accept the need to import crucial aspects of the employment relationship and determined instead to strike out on their own.

Thus the decline of multi-employer industrial relations arrangements accelerated significantly in the 1980s and 1990s. Industries where national agreements were abandoned altogether include engineering, newspaper printing and distribution, independent television, cement manufacturing and the clearing banks. Industries where the national-level agreement continues but where major companies within the sector have withdrawn include multiple food retailing and clothing and textiles. Alongside these developments, many firms that previously stood aloof from multi-employer arrangements with their own firm-wide agreements have broken up these arrangements and divisionalised them down to business unit level.

The same trends have been manifested in the public sector as shown, for example, by:

■ The breaking away of some local authorities from national negotiations.
■ The granting by the government of delegated freedom for new agencies to design their own grading and payment systems.
■ The ending of national pay negotiations in the railway industry following the break up of BR.

So we can see a clear move by employers to create space within which to mould the employment relationship to the requirements of their businesses. This process of internalisation is a necessary, but not a sufficient, condition for the move to a coherent, all-embracing reshaping of employment systems and relationships. In later chapters we will examine whether British employers have actually used the space which they have created in order to do the things which strategic HRM would have them do.

WHAT ABOUT THE WORKERS?

What is it like to be on the receiving end of these pressures and changes? We have examined the unprecedented array of forces bearing down on the structure, style, management processes and culture of business organisations. As the account has proceeded we have drawn attention to many features of the cluster that impact on the relationship between the organisation and the people it employs. Some of these effects are direct – such as the widespread internalisation of contractual agreements. Others are indirect, but none the less significant in their impact – such as the growing stress on quality and flexibility.

How can we construct the balance sheet? How should we set about calculating the extent to which these forces contribute positively to the experience of going to work, or conversely represent a deterioration in the quality of working life?

Certainly what we termed the 'new paradigm' of work and organisations contains within it many features that we would expect to find on the positive side of any such balance sheet. The emphasis on teamworking, and the rejection of hierarchical and bureaucratic structures are attractive (unless, of course, you are an unreconstructed bureaucrat or status-driven individual). The value ascribed to trust, openness, respect and listening – the notion that, as Tom Peters has it, the answer is much more likely to lie in the head of the production worker than in the plan of a middle manager – these all stand in refreshing, liberating even, contrast with the more traditional division between officers and other ranks that has been the daily experience of working life for the millions down the years. Is this not a prize to cherish – compensation in abundance for any disruption and turbulence that the process of change might bring and for the expectation of ever higher standards of performance that seem to be the other side of the trade-off?

'Well, up to a point', might come the reply. An alternative view might come from either of two directions. First, it could be argued that such an account presents a hopelessly naive and idealised view of life because it concentrates on espoused values and 'blue sky' futurology and ignores the crucial dimension of power. The employment contract, after all, still defines the relationship between the employer and the employed, and that can hardly be described as an agreement between two equals. Chapter 5 will document the many ways in which the legal rights of the individual worker have been curtailed since 1979, and the even more numerous ways in which the law has been changed to the detriment of the organisations which exist to redress the imbalance in the contractual relationship – trade unions. The point is succinctly captured by senior human resource practitioner Alan Fowler: 'Is it really possible to claim full mutuality when at the end of the day the employer can decide unilaterally to close the company or sell it to someone else?'[15] Second, we might, more simply, question the accuracy of the account as a believable description of how, in practice, most organisations are likely to behave towards their workforce.

The recession has yielded plenty of examples of fairly unrecon-structed managerial behaviour towards staff. Even without that source of pressure, however, it seems legitimate at least to question the extent to which British managerial attitudes – so long regarded as a major contributor to the class-ridden and conflict-strewn nature of our industrial life – have undergone a complete trans-formation. How serious have British managers actually been in their pursuit of the positive side of the balance sheet? Many clearly have meant it and have acted upon it. Can we not, however, in many other cases detect the continuing presence of the 'officers and other ranks' attitude underneath all the 'facilitating' and 'empowering' talk: a sense that the positive aspects of the new paradigm are there for their enjoyment while the pain is for the others, that 'flexibility' after all does mean two-tier employment?

We shall see. This is the question that lies at the heart of this book and which successive chapters will probe from different angles. The next chapter concerns the way in which the process of change is perceived and experienced at the place of work. Having explored the 'what' and the 'why' of change we turn to the 'how'. What do the dominant models tell us about the impact of change in the workplace and on the way in which people are managed? And what, again, can we glean about the reality behind the models?

References

1. Dertouzos, M L, Lester, R K and Solow, R M (1989) *Made in America*, The MIT Press, Cambridge, Mass., p 130
2. Channon, D (1980) 'Industrial structure', *Long Range Planning*, 15, p 10
3. Atkinson, J (1984) 'Manpower strategies for the flexible firm', *Personnel Management*, August
4. Pollert, A (1988) 'The flexible firm: A model in search of reality, or a policy in search of practice', *Warwick Papers in Industrial Relations*, no 19, University of Warwick, Warwick
5. Handy, C (1989) *The Age of Unreason*, Arrow Books, London, p 71
6. Ibid. p 56
7. Ibid. p 92
8. Peters, T (1987) *Thriving on Chaos*, Macmillan, London, p 357
9. Ibid. p 359
10. Peters, T (1992) *Liberation Management*, Macmillan, London, p 45
11. Pascale, R (1990) *Managing on the Edge*, Penguin, Harmondsworth, p35.

12. Ibid. p 32
13. Ibid. p 31
14. Moss Kanter, R (1983) *The Change Masters*, George Allen and Unwin, London, p 358
15. Fowler, A (1985) 'Getting into Organisational Restructuring', *Personnel Management*, February

CHAPTER 3

Strategy and Change in the Workplace

INTRODUCTION

In the previous chapter we examined the strong business pressures for change that have been confronting organisations over the last decade and a half, and some of the most significant patterns of response that can be detected. We encountered the D words – decentralisation, divisionalisation, devolution and deregulation, and we sketched out what might be termed a new paradigm, or received wisdom, about the way a successful organisation should be and look.

We began to explore the likely implications of the spread of this new paradigm among ever-wider circles of managers for the way in which work within organisations is structured, performed and managed, although we noted the continuing gap between the espoused values of the 'new' organisation – particularly those to do with trusting, delegating to, and 'empowering' the workforce at large – and the everyday reality of the way in which millions of employees continue to be managed. Somewhere in the midst of these reflections we had our first encounter with the concept of strategic human resource management.

This chapter takes the story a stage further. The focus here is on how, given the general picture of the pressures for change, businesses actually set about analysing their own specific circumstances, determining what their response should be, and then setting out to implement it in practice, and on how this process manifests itself in the workplace.

The chapter begins by looking at a series of approaches to the design of strategy – indeed at different definitions of the term 'strategy' itself. We see how different strategic approaches can manifest themselves in very different ways inside the workplace.

We then focus in on the process of change that lies, in varying ways, at the heart of all of the frameworks for strategic management that we examine. We find that the most commonly used models of change management – the process by which organisations set out to transform themselves in pursuit of a new business strategy – make important, but often hidden, assumptions about the way in which people in the workplace will behave.

There is much talk about 'ownership', 'commitment' and 'empowerment' and rather less about the process of participation by which people might actually come to feel that ownership by helping to shape the direction to which they will be expected to commit themselves. This has something to do with the fact that many of the change management models, rightly, put line managers – and especially middle managers – centre-stage in the achievement of effective change, whether of the incremental or the transformational sort, and are much louder in the messages that they send to managers about 'actively' and 'robustly' managing staff performance than about the skills and managerial behaviours required to build, develop and then give real responsibility to a genuinely empowered workforce.

The missing dimension in these accounts is that of power: and in particular of the balance of power in the employment relationship. This is an essentially pluralist observation – in the terms set out in Chapter 1. The argument of this chapter is that there is a strong sense of pluralism under the skin of the most persuasive of the change management models – a requirement, one might even say, for organisations to behave in a pluralist fashion if they are to achieve successful transformation – but that in practice change management is often pursued in a top-down, unitarist way, largely because it is seen as a senior management exercise bound in the trappings of 'strategy'. The challenge therefore concerns how this perspective can be built into the way that organisations approach the management of strategic change.

COWS, DOGS, CATS AND STARS

Our starting point is to examine the various ways in which organisations set about designing their responses to the sort of business-based pressures identified in the previous chapter. One of the most enduring frameworks for this thinking process was first provided by the Boston Consulting Group in the guise of the growth/share matrix. A familiar feature of countless management courses and texts, the strength of the matrix – reproduced below – is that it speaks directly to the trend, identified in Chapter 2, for organisations to respond to competitive pressures by diversifying and divisionalising. The key concept then is of the organisation as a portfolio of different businesses, and the role of strategic management is to manage the composition of the portfolio to best effect.

The growth/share matrix, it is argued, helps organisations to engage in this process of portfolio planning by providing managers with a way of classifying business units in terms of their potential use or generation of cash. It is based on a set of assumptions.

■ The existence of an 'experience curve' which means that costs fall – and therefore profits rise – the more experience an organisation has in the production of a particular product or service,

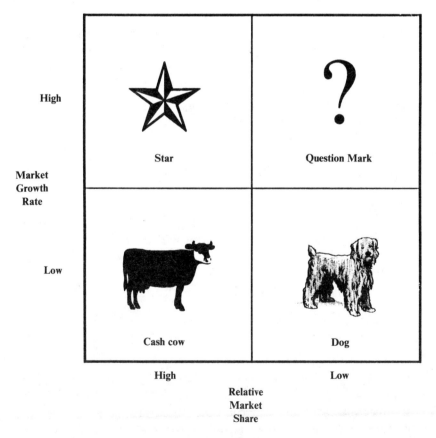

Figure 3.1 The growth/share matrix

which in turn comes from early entry and high market share relative to competitors.

■ Recognition that companies that are seeking to hold their share in growing markets will need more money for investment than those seeking to hold a share of more mature markets.

■ The importance of the life-cycle pattern of products, with successive stages of growth, maturity and decline, and the implication that it is easier for a firm to gain market share in the period of growth – when opportunities are widest – than when the product or service has matured.

By plotting market growth rate against market share the matrix produces four 'ideal types' of businesses.

■ *Cash cows.* These are businesses with a high share in a low growth market. They generate large profits and positive cash flow. They need only relatively small levels of investment to remain up to date and effectively functioning.

■ *Stars.* With a high relative share in a growth market, these businesses produce large profits – sufficient to finance future investment and to become the cash cows of the future. To reach a 'star' position, a business will require extensive investment – paid for by the current cash cows.

■ *Question marks (also known as wild cats).* Businesses with a low share of a high growth market could become profitable if they can move rapidly up the experience curve. Their situation is uncertain, however, and they will require investment in excess of their own profitability. They will be backed selectively – if they can gain market share before the market matures.

■ *Dogs.* With a low share of low growth markets, these are businesses without much of a future. The chances are that they will be sold or liquidated in order to raise some cash, or managed in such a way as to cut costs to the bare minimum and squeeze whatever revenue is possible out of them.

The thinking behind this model has been captured in the following terms:

> to create a pattern of capital spending whereby a business receives funding early in its life so that it achieves a strong (ie profitable) competitive position. Then, as its market matures the business will produce the cash flow that will fund other, more rapidly growing businesses ... (and) facilitate the creation of a portfolio of businesses in which the sources and uses of funds are nearly balanced.[1]

As we shall see shortly this can be readily challenged as a description of the way in which organisations actually plan their business. Nonetheless, the concept of 'portfolio planning' is sufficiently well rooted in management thinking as to make it credible that this sort of analysis will play at least some part in strategic business decisions. Moreover the framework serves to show neatly the way in which different market conditions can produce quite different constellations of business conditions – even within the same organisation.

As John Purcell has pointed out, this framework can also be used in order to examine the way in which organisations' responses to competitive business pressures are likely to impact on the way in which people within the organisation are employed and managed. He argues that employee relations needs are likely to differ substantially between the different segments of the growth/share matrix. Figure 3.2 summarises some of the key differences.

ALTERNATIVE APPROACHES TO STRATEGIC MANAGEMENT

As the preceding section has shown, the BCG growth/share matrix can help us to understand why the approaches of different organisations to the management of their employees should vary as extensively as they do. In particular it can help us to focus on the dimensions of the likely *changes* in employment practice arising from changes in business conditions that alter the position of a business unit within the portfolio of a particular organisation. At the same time, however, many have questioned the extent to which the matrix provides a valid account of the way in which organisations either do or should undertake strategic management. It has been pointed out, for example, that the model focuses entirely on short-term cash and asset management and completely ignores such key dimensions as the culture and distinctive competencies of the organisation. It has also been argued that the model suggests that there can be only one leader in any one market and that since, by implication, the only profitable position to be in is that of leader, 'ultimately companies which were not leaders should be liquidated leaving only one competitor in each market.'[2]

Successive influential writers on business strategy have looked instead at the strategic drivers, or 'thrusts', that determine the responses of organisations to their competitive environment. For Michael Porter[3] there were five strategic drivers:

Stars

Key need: To manage transition from small, entrepreneurial concern to increasingly large, sophisticated business.

Policy Regime: Formal, flexible framework designed by human resource professionals but implemented by line managers.

Typical features: 'Market leader' policy on pay; heavy investment in recruitment and training. Performance appraisal and performance related pay. Emphasis on teamwork and communications. Either no trade union or 'greenfield site' model: single union, no strike/arbitration etc arrangements.

Employee relations style: Heavy stress on flexibility, skill development and change management. Individualistic employment policies with emphasis on personal and group performance. Investment in human capital to match physical capital.

Question Marks

Key need: Management space and flexibility to determine prospects of the business and respond quickly when decision made on its future.

Policy Regime: Avoidance of formalised approaches, emphasis on fluidity, flexibility, innovation, etc.

Typical features: No formal grading structure, 'spot salaries' – market linked. Project group as unit of organisation: mobility, flexibility, skill acquisition.

Employee relations style: Great emphasis on informality, team working and status-free relationships. Meritocratic and individualistic. Collective forms of representation seen as 'alien' and irrelevant.

Cash cows

Key need: Order, stability, predictability to ensure continuing profit for use elsewhere.

Policy Regime: Structured, organised, non-experimental.

Typical features: Collective bargaining, trade union recognition plus facilities for union representatives, job evaluation, workstudy.

Employee relations style: Elements of paternalism (social clubs, canteens etc) plus emphasis on harmonious working, keeping the peace etc. Personnel department and union representatives share interest in defending custom and practice and status quo.

Dogs

Key need: Strong management control to bring business to point where it can be sold, or to drive down costs to squeeze out additional profits.

Policy Regime: 'Hard' management, adversarial industrial relations linked to directive line management. Lack of interest in 'developmental' human resource policies.

Typical features: 'Ability to pay' as basis of remuneration. Drive for productivity through 'give back' or flexibility deals, failing which agreements are imposed. Absence of training etc. Voluntary redundancy arrangements plus period bouts of layoffs.

Employee relations style: 'Opportunistic milking' – communication by command, management by decree. Preoccupation with intensifications of work effort, reduction of 'surplus' labour and cutting staff overheads, welfare etc.

Figure 3.2 Business needs and employees relations style

Source: Purcell, J Impact of Corporate Strategy on HRM (1989) New Perspective on human resource management, ed Storey, J Routledge pp 77–79

- Competitive rivalry.
- Barriers to entry.
- Threat of substitutes.
- The power of buyers.
- The power of suppliers.

For Cliff Bowman,[4] managers typically see *four* strategic thrusts:

- Competing on price.
- Offering unique products/services.
- Cost control.
- Product/service development.

In terms of their impact on the workplace, these four strategies map pretty closely on to the accounts, respectively, of the 'dogs', 'stars', 'cash cows' and 'question marks' set out in Figure 3.1 above.

STRATEGY AND STRUCTURE

So far then we have looked at some main accounts of the broad strategies that organisations might adopt in response to the pressures for change identified in the previous chapter, and seen that to some extent statements about likely employment policy implications can be drawn out of the analysis of the different strategic options. The next step is to consider the impact on workplace relationships of organisational structure. What are the implications of different structures for the way in which people are employed and managed?

The starting point for this is not the over-simplistic nostrum that 'structure follows strategy', which conveys an over-tidy view of life. We start instead with a number of 'hypotheses' derived by Henry Mintzberg[5] from his research into the structure of organisations:

- The older the organisation, the more formalized its behaviour.
- Structure reflects the age of founding of the industry.
- The larger the organisation, the more elaborate its structure – that is, the more specialized its tasks, the more differentiated its units, and the more developed its administrative component.
- The larger the organisation, the larger the average size of its units.
- The larger the organisation, the more formalised its behaviour.

Mintzberg[6] goes on from these and other related hypotheses to present us with five broad types, or configurations, of organisational structure:

Simple structures	Dominated by the top of the organisation. Centralised decision making and direct supervision.
Machine bureaucracy	Characterised by standardisation of work processes and the extensive reliance on 'systems'.
Professional bureaucracy	Here it is the standardisation of skills that provides the prime coordinating mechanism, thus giving rise to more autonomy among operators.
Divisionalised form	Which we have seen to be a major vehicle for decentralisation. Authority is drawn down from the apex and activities are grouped together in units which are then managed according to their standardised outputs.
Adhocracy	Power is decentralised selectively to constellations of work that are free to coordinate within and between themselves by mutual adjustment.

Mintzberg describes the key features and dimensions of his five organisational types in some detail and in terms which enable us to make some important connections between organisational structure and the flavour of workplace relationships. Figure 3.3 below brings together the key elements from Mintzberg's analysis which help us to make these connections.

All of this leaves us asking 'yes, but...' questions. 'Yes, but when are organisations likely to develop in one direction rather than another?' 'Yes, but just how close is the association between the pursuit of particular strategies and the adoption of particular organisational forms, and in turn the implementation of particular employment policy regimes?' 'Yes, but isn't the really important thing the *way* in which a particular strategy or organisational form is implemented?'

We can move a little way further towards answering questions of this sort by considering Figure 3.4 below.

This figure draws heavily on Mintzberg's analysis. It suggests that organisational structure will in practice involve a set of compromises – in particular, compromises between the three 'ideal

	Simple structure	Machine Bureaucracy	Professional Bureaucracy	Divisionalised Focus	Adhocracy
ENVIRONMENT	Simple and dynamic; sometimes hostile	Simple & stable	Complex & stable	Relatively simple and stable; diversified markets	Complex and dynamic; sometimes disparate
AGE AND SIZE	Typically young and small (first stage)	Typically old & large	Varies	Typically old and very large (third stage)	Typically young
UNIT SIZE	Large	Large at bottom, small elsewhere	Large at bottom, small elsewhere	Large at top	Small throughout
POWER	CEO control; often owner managed	Technocratic and sometimes external control	Professional operator control	Middle-line control	Expert control
KEY COORDINATING MECHANISM	Direct supervision	Standardisation of work	Standardisation of skills	Standardisation of outputs	Mutual adjustment
PLANNING AND CONTROL SYSTEMS	Little planning	Action planning	Little planning and control	Much performance control	Limited action planning
FLOW OF DECISION MAKING	Top-down	Top-down	Bottom-up	Differentiated between HQ and divisional	Mixed, all levels
SPECIALISATION OF JOBS	Little specialisation	Much horizontal and vertical specialisation	Much horizontal specialisation	Some horizontal and vertical specialisation (between division and HQ)	Much horizontal specialisation
FORMALISATION OF BEHAVIOUR	Little formalisation. Organic	Much formalisation. Bureaucratic	Little formalisation. Bureaucratic	Much formalisation (within divisions). Bureaucratic	Little formalisation. Organic

Figure 3.3 Key features of organisation types

Source: Extracted from Table 12.1 'Structure in Fives', Henry Mintzberg

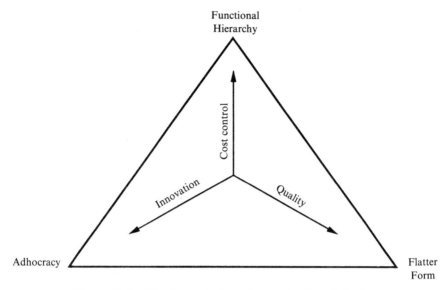

Figure 3.4   The boundaries of organisational design

types' represented, respectively by 'adhocracy', the functional hierarchy involved in the 'machine bureaucracy' or 'divisionalised form', and the flatter form of the 'professional bureaucracy'. Moreover, the point within this triangle of available compromises that an organisation chooses, will be determined by the relative strength of each of three forces that point towards different corners of the triangle:

■ *Cost control:* which points towards the grouping together of functions in order to minimise duplication and to strengthen lines of management information and control.
■ *Quality:* which points towards a flatter, less centralised structure within which responsibility for standards of service and production is spread more widely: quality is 'built in' by everyone rather than being 'inspected in' by supervisors and managers.
■ *Innovation:* which points towards the autonomy and creative informality of the adhocracy.

This would appear to show us two things. First, it shows us that there are sound, business-based reasons for the adoption of different organisational forms – that the 'flat and funky' paradigm characterised in the previous chapter will not be universally applicable. Second, and central to the concerns of this chapter, it seems to show us a structure or framework for thinking more systematically and less crudely about the relationships between business environment and strategy, on the one hand, and the organisation of work and management of people on the other. We can look *upstream* from the diagram to consider the linkages between competitive pressure, business strategy and organisational form, and *downstream* from it to consider the relationships between organisational form and key aspects of the management of the employment relationship.

We might expect, for example, that an organisation pursuing a strategy of cost control is, other things being equal, more likely to be structured in a top-down hierarchical form, with strong systems of work standardisation and supervision to ensure conformity with those systems, that it will be seeking aggressively to secure labour cost reductions through 'concession bargaining', 'flexibility deals' or straightforward imposition, and that it will be uninterested in skill formation or development among the workforce.

Conversely, we might expect the organisation pursuing a strategy of differentiating through quality, again, other things being equal, to have a flatter, more decentralised structure, to exhibit good channels of information – horizontally, as well as vertically – and a stress on teamworking, to have an infrastructure of quality management or customer service programmes and structures, and to have a professionalised employment policy regime, which may or may not include collective representation and bargaining, but will certainly have more individually-tailored arrangements in respect of performance management skill training and competence development.

STYLES

The observant reader will have spotted the underhand way in which the economist's weasel get-out phrase 'other things being equal' was slipped into the descriptions contained in the preceding two paragraphs! This is because it is necessary at this stage to enter some important qualifications to the use of the framework developed so far in this chapter. Other things are not, of course, equal. Organisations which are in similar market circumstances and have similar structures can still differ markedly in their values and behaviour. This difference relates very much to the *constraints* that are put on the otherwise seemingly rather free-floating business of choosing between particular organisational strategies and structures.

Prominent among the sources of such constraints lies the relationship between head offices and operating businesses. The way in which this relationship is managed determines the degree of freedom which operating units are given concerning their activities, management practices and policies.

Michael Goold and Andrew Campbell have analysed this issue and their research has led them to distinguish between two types of influence which corporate centres exert over business units. *Planning influence* 'concerns the centre's efforts to shape strategies as they emerge and before decisions are taken ... to improve the quality of thinking that surrounds major decisions'. *Control influence* on the other hand, 'arises from the targets that the centre agrees with its business units, the way the centre reacts to poor performance, and the frequency with which the centre monitors results'.[7]

By combining these two dimensions, Goold and Campbell[8] produce three principal styles governing the relationship between the corporate centre of an organisation and its component businesses. These are summarised in the following way:

- *Strategic planning*. The centre works with the business unit managers to develop strategy. It establishes extensive planning processes, makes contributions of substance to strategic thinking, and may have a corporate strategy or mission guiding and coordinating developments across the business units. Less attention is devoted to the control process. Performance targets are set in broader, more strategic terms such as 'become the leading supplier' or 'establish a position in'. Annual financial targets are seen as being less important than the longer term strategic objectives.
- *Financial control*. The centre's influence is exercised mainly through the budget process. Corporate management's role in developing strategies is limited, and long-term plans are not formally reviewed by the centre. Instead, the centre focuses on a close review of the annual budget. Profit targets are set when the budget is approved, and careers are at stake if budgets are missed. Financial control companies combine a low level of planning influence with tight financial controls.
- *Strategic control*. The centre prefers to leave the initiative in the development of plans to business unit managers. The centre does review and criticise the plans, but it uses reviews as a check rather than as an opportunity to give direction. The control

process is an important influence mechanism for the centre. targets are set for strategic objectives (such as market share) as well as financial performance, and managers are expected to meet the targets. Budgets can only be missed when important strategic objectives are at stake. Strategic Control companies combine moderate planning influence with tight strategic controls.

Two key points seem to emerge from this account. First, it is possible to draw some reasonably robust inferences about the sort of employment policy regimes that are likely to be associated with the three styles described above.

Thus, for example, the pressures on business unit managers in financial control companies to hit financial targets or face career consequences are likely to cascade down within the business unit in the form of strong control and supervision systems, a culture of discipline and conformance and a strong emphasis on rewarding the achievement of short-term objectives (or more likely, punishing their non-achievement).

Similarly, strategic planning companies seem much more likely to create the space within which individual business units can design and manage their own goals and targets, involving staff in the process of charting the strategic course and creating a sense of ownership, of shared commitment, to the strategy. It is not therefore surprising to find David Guest[9] arguing that only strategic planning companies have the capacity and commitment to develop human resource management as the basis for their employment policies.

The second key point to arise from Goold and Campbell's analysis is that we are presented with a third variable to help determine an organisation's approach to the organisation of work and the management of the employment relationship. We have already looked at the choice of broad competitive strategy (price-leadership, differentiation on quality etc), and at the design of organisational structure as powerful shapers of workplace life. Here we have a third, and at least partially-independent variable – the style of the relationship between the centre and individual units – also influencing the outcome.

THE HUMAN FACTOR

What we have so far helps us to analyse the likely impact of particular strategies or structures, or corporate relationships on employment relations once they have been adopted. It will not serve us very well when we are trying to predict how an organisation is likely to set about changing itself in response to business pressures. Nor will it be sufficient as a guide to how organisations seek to implement change – especially when at the heart of their strategy is a set of assumptions about how people within the organisation should behave and carry out their jobs.

In many ways this takes us to the heart of a strong critique of many conventional accounts of business strategy and how it is formulated and carried through inside organisations. Never mind the grand designs, bold analytical statements and cool, clear-headed models, runs this argument. What actually counts is what people do in practice and, in particular, what managers do when, in 'default mode', they take decisions, allocate resources and manage people. That is the way in which the real or 'emergent' strategy of the organisation is revealed: read my deeds, not my lips!

This case has been very forcefully argued by Cliff Bowman and Gerry Johnson[10] in the following terms:

> Planning systems, even when they exist, may not be central to the formulation of strategy; strategic options often are not systematically analysed, and objectives may be ill-defined, diverse, post-rationalised, unstated or very generalised... None of this is to say that managers behave in irrational ways. The formulation of strategy is strongly influenced by what might loosely and positively be called managerial experience (or less positively, the received wisdom of management)... In effect, managers develop over time and through experience an understanding and interpretation of the context in which they operate, which they apply to the situations they face. In this sense there is a 'taken for grantedness' or 'presumed logic' brought to bear.
>
> It is an organisational view of the world which helps interpret the changes facing the organisation and the individual within it.

The 'paradigm' is portrayed in terms of a 'cultural web' that brings together commonly held views on 'the way things are done around here' with conventions regarding organisational structures and the power and control systems that underpin them, together with stories, myths, heroes and villains, that go a long way towards defining how things happen and how things ought to happen.

The argument then is that in the middle of the rational, logical strategic planning process, replete with SWOT analyses and market segmentation matrices, sits a filter of cognitive, experientially-based 'received wisdom' which sums up the way in which the managers of an organisation will tend to look at the world and what is possible and important within it.

Crucially we can also see that the 'cultural web' that goes to make up this filter will include strong assumptions about how people are best managed, about what motivates a workforce, about what constitutes 'fair' and 'reasonable' behaviour and about the legitimacy or otherwise of, for example, the recognition of trade unions as the representative voice of the workforce within the organisation.

The significance of this cultural dimension can be seen, for example, in the very different labour relations approaches adopted by inwardly-investing companies from different countries. The Japanese companies investing in South Wales have shown a distinctive approach – and one that was more open to dealing with trade unions (albeit in a tightly defined way) than, say, their American counterparts. Many of these latter, on the other hand, have shown a stronger commitment to the values of HRM than has been the norm among indigenous UK companies.

It is therefore misleading to conceive of the process of deciding strategy as being distinct from the process of implementation. They are part of a continuous process, and the thread that runs through the process is a paradigm that both helps to interpret the outside world and its threats and possibilities to the organisation, but also moulds the organisation's view about how people behave, and what is an appropriate basis on which to manage and employ them.

MANAGING CHANGE, AND CHANGING WORK

This description seems more appropriate to the more turbulent economic conditions of the 1990s, in which the ability continuously to scan the changing scene and to reposition the organisation within it is of prime importance. In that context it is not surprising that so much importance has been ascribed to the *management of change* as a source of competitive advantage – indeed of survival.

A useful starting point is the three-stage 'unfreezing' model widely used in public and private sector alike, and which addresses the importance of the 'paradigm', or cultural web, discussed in the previous section. In this model actions are taken and programmes put in place to 'unfreeze' people within the organisation, to put aside long-held beliefs and values and become receptive to a new way of operating and, indeed, of looking at the world.

We might readily find this approach to change being used in, say, a manufacturing concern seeking to shift the emphasis away from an output- or production-centred view of the world and towards one in which product quality is prioritised. It might be an insurance company seeking to shake off its actuarily-rooted concern with risk avoidance in favour of an emphasis on marketing new, comprehensible (to the consumer that is) products, or in a civil service department moving away from a strong tradition of hierarchical working and the supremacy of the policy maker towards a 'diamond-shaped' organisation and a stress on commercial skills.

In each case the change management prescription would be the same: unfreeze people from their existing paradigm, teach them new ways of thinking and behaving, and then consolidate the new ways by refreezing people into a new paradigm. This is an interesting model, not only because it is so commonly used, but also because it has such clear implications for the way in which people are to be managed within the organisation.

In terms of the distinction drawn in Chapter 1, this is a highly unitarist approach. The shift in paradigm which is deemed to be necessary is determined at the top of the organisation (or indeed from outside the organisation) and the succeeding stages of the process involve the rest of the organisation being led to understand the inappropriateness of their long-held beliefs and adopting the new 'mindset'. There is little if any scope here for the maverick, for the sceptic, or for recognising that different opinions may be legitimately held within the workforce, in the way implied by the pluralist outlook. The commitment required from the workforce is commitment to an externally designed view of their world.

Something of the same sense can also be found in other, more systematic models of change management which aim to take full account of the importance of the external business environment, as well as of the internal paradigm, or received wisdom. These other models share some important features. They each display a rational, logical framework in which the outside world is analysed/interpreted and in which, within an overall strategy, different 'levers' are pulled at different levels. They each have a sense of change as something which is done by senior people in an organisation to people at the levels below them. They are long on the need for commitment and short on scope for involving employees in the design and determination of the overall direction of change. They are also relatively short on accounts of what the 'glue' will be when the change has been made and needs to be sustained in the longer term.

MANAGING CHANGE: WHAT MANAGERS ACTUALLY DO

In the light of these comments, it is interesting to look at an approach to classifying strategies for change first developed in the early 1970s by Keith Thurley.[11] The usefulness of his approach is that it brings into the change management picture a consideration of the power relationships between the actors involved in the change process.

Thurley describes five 'ideal type' basic approaches to carrying through changes. These are characterised in terms of the sequence in which they work through the stages of changes, and also of the style and method of implementation which they are likely to involve. The five approaches are:

■ Directive.
■ Bargained.
■ Normative (or hearts and minds).
■ Analytical.
■ Action-based.

The *directive* approach involves the imposition of change, even where this involves the by-passing of established procedures for consulting or involving staff. (Indeed switching from a consultative to a directive mode may be a deliberate move in order to send a message about the seriousness of the situation as seen by the organisation's senior managers.) This approach is often to be found when time is seen as being of the essence in carrying through changes – to the extent that involvement or consultation is seen as a 'luxury' that can no longer be afforded and other approaches to change management are ruled out. The directive approach is also often to be found when other less-coercive approaches have been tried and either are seen to have failed, or senior managers have simply lost patience with the time and processes involved and have reverted to a style of management with which they feel instinctively more comfortable.

The *bargained* approach is also about power, but epitomises the pluralist concept in which power is seen as shared between the employer and the employed and in which, therefore, the process of change requires negotiation, compromise and agreement between the two sides as the basis for moving forward.

The *normative*, or *hearts and minds* approaches refer to the type of unfreezing/freezing model described above and indeed other 'big programme' change activities. As we have seen there is a strong unitarist strain running through such approaches – an all-embracing attitude to the need to change the attitudes, values and beliefs of the entire workforce. A point to note about this approach is that, because of its comprehensive nature, it is likely to involve the most widespread rewriting of the terms and conditions contained in the formal contracts of employment within the organisation, and the most fundamental reshaping of the informal or psychological contract. Yet most normative accounts of change management say little or nothing about the practical, contractual underpinning necessary in order to freeze the new paradigm and sustain the change once it has been achieved. 'Commitment' and 'shared vision' seem to be the prime candidates on offer to provide this glue: there is little discussion of the need for involvement and participation if commitment is to be forthcoming.

The *analytical* approach to change is a very theoretical account of the change process. It proceeds sequentially from the analysis and diagnosis of the situation, through the setting of objectives and design and implementation of change programmes and on to the evaluation of the results and the determination of the objectives for the next stage in the change process. It is rational, logical in its sequencing, evaluative and therefore in principal capable of being open-minded towards ideas for change from all parts of the organisation. Life of course is seldom, if ever, like this, although many an otherwise chaotic change programme may proceed from a rational first vision of the desired direction of change and may incorporate rational and analytical elements.

Thurley's final 'ideal type', the *action-based* approach to the management of change, speaks directly to the widely-observed fact that the way in which managers behave in practice bears little relation to the analytical, theoretical model. The line between managerial thought and managerial action blurs in practice to the point of invisibility: what managers think is what they do. And since managers are constantly required to hop between different timeframes and juggle an ever-more complex set of priorities, real life will tend to favour the 'ready, fire, aim' approach to change management. The strategy starts from a vague understanding of the problem, but the process of trying out experimentally-different solutions both clarifies the nature of the problem and moves the organisation towards a shared understanding of what is likely to constitute an appropriate solution – or, more likely, an appropriate framework within which solutions might be discovered.

The action-based approach to change chimes very closely with an influential argument put forward by Beer, Eisenstat and Spector in the *Harvard Business Review* under the title: 'Why change programmes don't produce change'.[12] Their argument was that change programmes that are company-wide and directed from the top and sponsored by staff departments are unlikely to work, just as trying to change people's behaviour by changing their attitudes is unlikely to succeed. Instead the key to successful change is seen to lie in work-related projects, usually in a specific area and in putting people in 'a new organisational context'.

The focus is on the very concrete concept of 'task alignment' rather than on abstract notions such as 'culture change', and on starting the process of change at the periphery and working steadily in towards the centre, rather than trying to drive everything out from the centre or down from the top. Indeed the role of the top of the organisation in respect of change programmes is a facilitating one: to create a climate for change and then to help spread the lessons to be drawn from successful (and indeed unsuccessful) local change initiatives sideways through the rest of the organisation.

The six steps on the critical path of an effective change programme, as proposed in the article, are:

1. Mobilise commitment through a joint diagnosis of business problems.
2. Develop a shared vision of how to organise and manage for competitiveness.
3. Foster a consensus for the new vision, the competence to enact it and the cohesion to move it along.
4. Spread revitalisation to all departments without pushing it from the top: 'it's better to let each department reinvent the wheel'.
5. Institutionalise revitalisation through formal policies, systems and structures.
6. Monitor and adjust strategies in response to problems in the revitalisation process: 'learn how to learn'.

'BUT WHAT DOES IT MEAN FOR ME?'

Two points stand out concerning this approach. First it is shot through with a far more genuine commitment to the 'democratic' aspects of 'empowerment' and 'involvement' than is the norm with other models of change management. There is no shortage of approaches that make much of the central importance of the 'people factor' in managing successful change, but which under pressure default to a top-down mode of seeking to implement centrally-determined changes through cascades of information communiques, team briefings and new procedure manuals. Here, to the contrary, we find an approach that calls upon organisations to have the courage to 'let go', to give staff real responsibility for designing and implementing changes that will affect the way they work and interact with the rest of the organisation – even to the point (horror!) of making mistakes.

The second point is that the proposed approach recognises the need for formal processes, systems and structures to institutionalise the process of revitalisation, thus rectifying the omission noted above in models that are strong on the clarion call for change but weak on describing the things that are going to be put in place to sustain the change, to make it a reality in people's daily lives.

In employee relations terms this seems to be a point of considerable importance, but one that is frequently underplayed or even ignored completely by those who focus on 'change management' as primarily a top management activity, rooted in a top-down and unitarist conception of strategic management. What emerges instead is a model of the successfully-changing organisation that advances by giving real authority and power to groups within it to experiment, to argue, to make mistakes, and to learn: all within a framework of facilitation – not control – by the top.

The implication is that it is open to groups of employees to contribute their own ideas about how their work can most effec-tively be structured, organised and managed and that they should be given considerable freedom to try their ideas out in practice. A quasi-pluralist, at least, tolerance of different ideas and prescrip-tions is implied, as well as a respect for employees, irrespective of level or status. As we shall see in later chapters there is nothing in here which is by definition inimical to the existence of trade unions, or indeed to their playing a role in the revitalisation process, (although as we shall see in the next chapter this will present unions with some significant challenges), even though the model can operate perfectly well without them.

Reflecting on the position of trade unions in the change management model does, however, lead on to the second and critical employee relations point. Yes, employees are empowered by the kind of approach advocated by Beer and his colleagues – but managers are even more strongly empowered. Not only that, they are positively enjoined to experiment, to take risks, to be more entrepreneurial, to fire without aiming, and to do so moreover in ways that will bear directly on the employment position and contractual terms of the managed workforce. Here is a dilemma. On the one hand the dynamic approach to change management seems to demand the sort of flexible approach to the definition of roles and responsibilities captured in Handy's 'fried egg' device, discussed in Chapter 2. On the other, it puts the spotlight on the quality of the relationship between manager and staff. 'How boring of my staff', thinks the thrusting, learning-by-doing, change-minded manager, 'to want revised job descriptions and updated contracts'. 'How flakey', think his/her staff, 'to be going on about changing the way we do things around her the whole time, but not to be able to describe it precisely in terms of what exactly we are supposed to be doing'.

TRUST AND THE EMPLOYMENT RELATIONSHIP

There are several valid ways of responding to this dilemma (the approach which is not valid – but which is far too commonly found – is to deny its existence). One is to focus in tight on the importance of trust in the conduct of the relationship between manager and managed, employer and employed, and of what is involved in gaining it and keeping it. There are echoes here of the distinction made twenty years ago by Alan Fox of 'high trust' and 'low trust' systems of industrial relations.[13]

What seems to be required here is a for a high degree of trust to exist in the employment relationship. Sufficiently high, for example, that employees are prepared to allow the formal constraints of employment contracts to be relaxed or renegotiated enough to allow managers to try out new ways of managing – on the basis that the trust implied by this will not be abused and that the result will not be what Lord McCarthy[14] described as the exercise of the right to manage 'in the sense of managers consulting nobody but themselves before taking irreversible decisions affecting the future employment and well-being of their staff'. On the other hand, it requires managers to trust groups of staff sufficiently to allow them the opportunity and the power to experiment with ways of working that might mark quite radical departures for the organisation.

The pressure that this puts on organisations to be consistent is considerable: not to be rational or logical, but to be consistent in the pursuit of high trust relations. There really is not a half-way house along the road to 'empowerment' and involvement. There certainly is not room for the kind of flip-flopping between participative or even 'Hearts and minds' approaches, and unilateral direction and coercion, which has been something of a feature of recent practice. Once an organisation sets out on this route (and by no means all will want to, need to, or be able to) it has to mean it, and be seen to mean it.

It also has to be pretty clear about what the structures, systems and processes (to use Beer's phrase) are which it intends to put in place in order to institutionalise the process of revitalisation and bring it to life in terms of daily working reality for those employed in the organisation. In this regard we have already had a series of encounters with the concept of human resource management as the last two chapters have proceeded. It is time to take a closer look, and to assess whether it is going to provide us with the glue to hold the concept of strategic change and of change management together. That is the business of the next chapter.

References

1. Hamermesh, R G (1986) *Making Strategy Work: How Senior Managers Produce Results*, Wiley, New York, p 16
2. Pitt-Watson, D (1992) 'Business Strategy and Economics', in Faulkner, D, and Johnson, G, *The Challenge of Strategic Management*, Kogan Page, London, p 46
3. Porter, M (1980) *Competitive Strategy*, The Free Press, New York, Macmillan
4. Bowman, C (1992) 'Charting corporate strategy', in Faulkner, D and Johnson, G *op. cit.* p 65
5. Mintzberg, H (1983) *Structure in Fives*, Prentice Hall International, Englewood Cliffs, NJ, pp 123–35
6. Ibid. p 153

7. Goold, M and Campbell, A (1987) *Strategies and Styles*, Basil Blackwell, Oxford, pp 36–40
8. Ibid. pp 42–3
9. Guest, D (1987) 'Human resource management and industrial relations', *Journal of Management Studies*, 24, p 518
10. Bowman, C and Johnson, G (1992) 'Surfacing corporate strategy', in Faulkner, D and Johnson, G *op. cit.* pp 180–81
11. Thurley, K (1979) *Supervision: A Reappraisal*, Heinemann, London
12. Beer, M, Eisenstat, E and Spector, B (1990), 'Why change programmes don't produce change', *Harvard Business Review*, Nov/ Dec, p 158
13. Fox, A (1974) *Beyond Contract: Work, Power, and Trust Relations*, Faber & Faber, London
14. McCarthy, W E J and Ellis, N D (1973) *Management by Agreement*, Hutchinson & Co, London, p 94

CHAPTER 4

Human Resource Management

INTRODUCTION

So far we have examined some of the principal structural changes that have reshaped the environment for business organisations, and we have looked at various ways in which these and related changes have fed through to the way in which we look at the world of work.

We have seen how these changes have made themselves felt in the workplace and the various ways in which the change process has been managed. We have noted the significance of the drive by employers – supported by changes in the system of labour law – to respond to this new environment by *internalising* their employee relations: creating structures, rules and processes that are tailored to the specific circumstances of the organisation (and indeed, where possible, of the individual business unit within it), and are insulated from 'external' influences and organisations.

This is the context for examining the phenomenon of 'human resource management' (HRM). Setting aside the sometimes imprecise definitions of HRM, there is a general sense in which it is seen as providing increasingly the basis for the regulation of employee relations in this ever more internalised world of work – and thereby as displacing the collectively-based conduct of industrial relations.

In this chapter therefore we shall be taking a close look at HRM, and in particular at the concept of strategic HRM. We shall be asking what is new about it. We shall examine the evidence that is available from surveys and academic studies on the extent to which it has taken root in the practice of UK organisations, and on the forces that have been most instrumental in determining both the extent and the actual shape of HRM in Britain.

SOME DEFINITIONS

Accounts of HRM are often presented in quite dramatic terms, as if it represents a fundamental break with past practice. In its extreme form the argument runs that there has been a change of paradigm – of the commonly accepted model of how things are done. Out with union-dominated and compromise-riddled industrial relations and in with individualistic and strategically-oriented human resource management! Away with the obstructive and bureaucratic personnel department and in with the business-driven and 'can do' human resource function. There is also frequently a touch of triumphalism and of missionary zeal here:[1]

> Yet within the decade, the balance had been pushed back again. No more beer and sandwiches in Downing Street, record *low* numbers of strikes, falling union membership, rising recriminations in the TUC, the ghostworking and restrictive practices of Fleet Street lying abandoned... For the changing shape of our economy has made the traditional divide between the 'two sides' of industry as irrelevant now as it was sterile before; today's manager must harness the individuality of his workforce, recognise the motivational importance of raising product quality, and create the team spirit to achieve it. In this environment – in many cases a post-union environment – a new style of management must evolve.

In this one short passage we can find many of the strands that must be disentangled in order to reach an understanding of the nature and scope of HRM today, and of its likely evolution in the future:

■ A focus on individualism rather than collectivism as the basis of employment relationships.
■ An assumption that the rise of HRM is the reverse side of the coin from the decline of trade unionism.
■ Placing the rise of HRM firmly in the context of new production techniques – especially those that are based on improving product quality.
■ An association between the spread of human resource management practices and the development of an increasingly 'unitarist' account of the relationship between employer and employed, at the expense of a 'pluralist' view that recognised the existence of certain legitimate fundamental divergences of interest between the 'two sides'.
■ A tendency to elide description with exhortation: to run together, in other words, factual accounts of changes that have

been made to management practice and a vision of the changes that are required in order to usher in an ideal state.

This last point leads on to a wider difficulty when it comes to getting to grips with what actually are the distinguishing features of HRM. As Storey has pointed out, there is a considerable danger of 'contrasting an idealised version of HRM with a practical lived-in account of the messy reality of personnel management'.[2]

Storey begins his own account of the distinctive features of HRM with the following classification of the different meanings attached to the phrase:[3]

1. As a synonym for personnel management – either loosely in order to substitute for other, equally loose, usages ('people management', 'employee relations' etc), or in a rather shallow way to give a more 'modern' ring to unchanged practices.

2. As a signal that the various techniques of personnel management are being/ought to be used in a more integrated way so that performance is improved through a 'cycle' of strategic human resource interventions covering, sequentially, selection, appraisal, reward and development

3. As a description of a more business-oriented and business-integrated approach to the management of labour, approached in the same way as other resources – capital, land, energy, technology etc – as having the potential to raise the performance and profitability of the organisation, rather than representing a problem area which can, at best, be neutralised.

4. As an approach to the management of people which is qualitatively different: not only are HR interventions firmly linked in to a wider business strategy, but they 'look and feel different'. This may well be because they are focused on the pursuit of employee commitment rather than the more traditional Tayloristic search for compliance and control.

Not surprisingly, given these very different types of meaning attached to apparently the same concept, the net result is often a certain amount of confusion. Storey puts the point this way:[4]

What is striking is that the same term is thus capable of signalling diametrically opposite sets of assumptions. Hence, some observers are found objecting to the term 'human resources' because it smacks of an 'instrumental' treatment of people, while other critics are inclined to dismiss it for a very different reason, namely, that it suggests a wishy-washy, liberal approach which, they say, however much we may lament the fact, is simply inappropriate to the harsh realities of business.

We have also noted a third, more cynical reaction: that the term is objectionable because it is, at root, a piece of jargon purporting to be new but in fact providing a smokescreen behind which personnel managers and industrial relations departments have simply re-labelled themselves.

One further point to underline concerns the two quite distinctive senses in which the word 'integration' appears in the second and third category of meaning quoted above. In the second category the emphasis is very much on the integration of different aspects of HRM in order to produce internal consistency in the execution of the various policies. Thus, for example, there would be a strong concern here to ensure that selection took place on the basis of criteria (or perhaps a set of competencies) which in turn related to the attributes contained in the appraisal system, and also to the process of identifying future training and development needs. The strategic purpose underlying the reward system in this scenario is to ensure that the messages which the organisation wishes to give to staff through the appraisal system are reinforced through the tangible evidence of the pay packet, (and also to ensure that employees are not deflected from the pursuit of development goals of long-term importance by a payment system that focuses them entirely on short term objectives – or, say, on the pursuit of quantity of output rather than quality of service).

In the third category the sense attached to the term 'integration' has shifted. Here the emphasis is on the linking up of human resource policies to the wider business strategy of the organisation. Human resource policies are judged to be valid in so far as they can be traced directly back to specific aspects of the business strategy and can be seen to give direct support to the strategy's implementation. This also has the effect of widening the ambit of strategic HRM beyond the traditional boundaries of personnel practice and to include areas such as the design of organisational structures most likely to support the business strategy and the management of corporate culture which, on this reading, comes to be seen as a separate, overarching force making for integration, cohesiveness and compliance with corporate objectives.

The significance of the distinction between these different uses of the term 'integration' is that they can pull us in different directions. The result can be a tension between the pressure on the HR professional to create, and then to protect, a neat cycle of mutually reinforcing policies and the countervailing pressure to show the agility to react nimbly to the effects of the shocks on the business from an ever more chaotic outside world, and to live with the inevitably resulting ambiguity.

OLD WINE IN NEW BOTTLES?

If we accept Storey's account of the different meanings attached to the term 'human resource management' we should be clear that it is the last three categories (and the last two in particular) with which we are concerned here. In other words the interest lies in analysing the developments that appear to be new – assessing the extent to which they actually are new, and investigating the implications for present and future management practice.

Michael Armstrong has put forward what he sees as four fundamental principles on which HRM is based:[5]

1. People are the most important assets an organisation has and their effective management is the key to its success.
2. Organisational success is most likely to be achieved if the personnel policies and procedures of the enterprise are closely linked with, and make a major contribution to, the achievement of corporate objectives and strategic plans.
3. The corporate culture and the values, organisational climate and managerial behaviour emanating from that culture will exert a major influence on the achievement of excellence. This culture must be managed, which means that strong pressure, starting from the top, needs to be exerted to get the values accepted and acted upon.
4. Continuous effort is required to encourage all the members of the organisation to work together with a sense of common purpose. It is particularly necessary to secure commitment to change.

The next question is the extent to which this describes an approach which is genuinely new from the respective viewpoints of the workforce, personnel management professionals, industrial relations specialists and, indeed, the wider management community.

Karen Legge set out to answer this question and found that many of the aspects of HRM that are claimed to be innovative can be found in long-standing accounts of the role that should be performed by the personnel function. She identified the following significant points of similarity:[6]

1. Both models emphasise the importance of integrating personnel/HRM practices with organisational goals. Particularly in the case of the American commentators it cannot even be said that the language has changed.
2. Both models vest personnel/HRM firmly in line management.
3. Both models, in the majority of instances, emphasise the importance of individuals fully developing their abilities for their own personal satisfaction and to make their 'best contribution' to organisational success.
4. Both models identify placing the 'right' people into the 'right' jobs as an important means of integrating personnel/HRM practice with organisational goals.

She does, however, identify three key differences between the two models:

1. Whereas personnel management is largely seen as a management activity aimed at non-managers, HRM has a particularly strong focus on the development of the 'management team'.
2. HRM gives much greater responsibility to line managers – moving beyond personnel management's sense of devolving responsibility for the implementation of a set of personnel policies that are still for the most part centrally determined to a position in which line managers are seen as business managers responsible for coordinating and directing *all* resources in the business unit in pursuit of bottom-line results.
3. Most HRM models emphasise the management of the organisation's culture as the central activity for senior management.

Reasoning along similar lines, Alan Fowler concluded that 'the real difference between HRM and personnel management is not what it is, but who is saying it. In a nutshell HRM represents the discovery of personnel management by chief executives'.[7]

HRM AND INDUSTRIAL RELATIONS

Having looked at the similarities and differences between HRM and personnel management we now turn to the relationship between HRM and industrial relations. Storey again gives a useful starting point:[8]

> The classic definitions of industrial relations refer to it as 'the making and administering of rules which regulate employment relationships' and declare the focus of its study to be 'the institutions of job regulation'; but what is distinctive about HRM ... is that it

eschews the joint regulative approach – and even more so the craft regulative approach. It is impatient of custom and practice, of the going rate, of parity, mutuality, of rule books and procedure manuals, of deferring to personnel and IR specialists. In their place the various initiatives which might, for convenience sake, be denoted as HRM, place emphasis on utilising labour to its full capacity or potential. HRM is therefore about (and the term is used neutrally here) *exploiting* the labour resource more fully.

David Guest, who was an early analyst of the distinctive features of HRM in a UK context, has analysed the impact which the adoption of HRM techniques might have on an organisation's industrial relations, starting from the premiss that:[9]

> [t]he driving force behind the introduction of HRM appears to have very little to do with industrial relations; rather, it is the pursuit of competitive advantage in the market place through provision of high-quality goods and services, through competitive pricing linked to high productivity and through the capacity swiftly to innovate and manage change in the market place or to breakthroughs in research and development.

His conclusions are that:

- HRM values are unitarist to the extent that they assume no underlying and inevitable differences of interest between management and workers.
- HRM values are essentially individualistic and seek to avoid operating through group and representative systems. 'Both the formal and the psychological contracts for shop-floor workers are more akin to those typically offered to managers'.
- HRM is not necessarily anti-union but its practice (partly because of the foregoing points) poses considerable challenges to trade unionism.
- In particular, HRM will tend to see little scope for collective representation or collective bargaining, will exert pressure on employees to choose between their loyalty to their trade union and their allegiance to the firm and, at least in theory may, by raising the quality of management, reduce the case for trade unions as protective devices against arbitrary and unfair management.
- Even where the practice of HRM does not take an overtly anti-union form it may very well be introduced through policies that tend to bypass the union (as we shall see this may even in some instances be a prime motivation for the introduction of HRM).

Finally, Guest reminds us that if HRM poses a challenge to trade unionism it poses an equally (arguably even more) onerous challenge to managers.[10] In particular it:

> presents a major challenge to management competence and to the ability of management to sustain the quality of performance necessary to prevent issues arising which provide fertile ground for union activity. In many cases, more especially in workplaces where the unions are already well established and the system of management and control is built on more traditional adversarial assumptions about management–employee relations it is likely to prove extremely difficult for management to rise to this challenge.

In later chapters we will look in some detail at the extent to which managers have risen to this challenge.

The final point to note in connection with the argument about whether HRM represents a substantially new departure or conversely the latest piece of faddish management jargon, is a distinction drawn by Storey, but used more widely, between what he terms 'hard' and 'soft' versions of HRM. It is a distinction that helps account for the, at first sight, confusing differences in reaction that the phrase 'human resource management' can engender.

'Soft' HRM is used to denote an approach that very much emphasises the 'human resource' part of the phrase. The 'soft' version traces its roots to the human-relations school; it emphasises communication, motivation and leadership. The 'hard' version, conversely, emphasises the quantitative, calculative and business-strategic aspects of managing the headcount resource in as 'rational' a way as for any other factor. The stress here is on the 'management' of the human resource and there is a strong implication that different groups of managers, and indeed different functional specialisms, are prone to come down heavily in favour of this, rather than the other version, of the term. This useful distinction will be kept in mind in the next section, where we look at the evidence behind the rhetorical claims for the spread of HRM.

THE REALITY BEHIND THE RHETORIC

So far then we have looked at the range of ways in which HRM has been defined and at some of the key conceptual differences between HRM as a model, and the corresponding accounts of personnel management and industrial relations. Now the task is to assess the extent to which we can find evidence for the adoption of the HRM model on the ground.

The distinguishing hallmarks of human resource management for which we are looking are those suggested by David Guest:[11]

■ Flexibility among employees.
■ High product and process quality.
■ High employee commitment.
■ Strategic integration.

By taking each feature in turn and assessing the extent to which it is or is not a growing feature of UK business practice we may get closer to a view of the reality of what has been going on inside organisations.

Flexibility

The search for improved employee flexibility was certainly one of the battle cries of the late 1980s, just as its counterpart – labour market flexibility – was a major component of government policy at the time. Some radical changes in working practices can indeed be seen to have taken place – typically involving some combination of:

■ Multi-skilling and multi-role working.
■ The replacement of job descriptions that define the boundaries of what an employee will be asked to do with an open-ended commitment on their part to do any work that they are equipped to perform.
■ Harmonisation of key terms and conditions between 'staff' and 'manual workers'.
■ The replacement of restrictions on working time and steep premia for overtime and shiftworking with flexible – sometimes annualised – working hours systems.

The driver for changes of this sort has, to a large extent, been the widespread adoption of new operating technologies, with their emphasis on short-run batch production and big reductions in set-up time. An indication of the prevalence of this sort of approach is contained in the Government-sponsored 1990 Workplace Industrial Relations Survey.[12]

■ Fully one-third of all workplaces in the survey had introduced more flexible working practices during the three years up to 1990.

■ This trend was reflected across the whole economy but was particularly strong in manufacturing sectors such as chemicals and clothing and in financial services and telecommunications.
■ Manual employees and non-manual employees were affected in equal measure across the whole economy.

So, evidence then for the widespread adoption of HRM as a distinctly new approach? A cynical view would dispute this, arguing instead that there is nothing new about the introduction of widespread changes in working practices and citing the successive waves of 'productivity bargaining' in the 1960s and 1970s as evidence that such changes are fully compatible with a traditional approach to industrial relations. There is some comfort for the holders of this view in the Workplace Survey[13] which found also that:

■ In 73 per cent of workplaces with recognised trade unions major changes were introduced on the basis of consultation with the union.
■ In some two-fifths of cases major changes had been made but there were still important limits reported by managers themselves on their own freedom to proceed unilaterally.

Such findings echo the conclusions drawn by the independent pay researchers, Incomes Data Services, from their review of cases of improved flexibility:[14] 'In many respects the aims of companies are no different from the late 1960s. The difference is that they are now investing in training.'

On the other hand three key points need to be set against attempts to play down the significance and scale of recent attempts to extend flexibility:

1. The greater than hitherto extent to which the drive for improved flexibility is taking place beyond the reach of trade unions – either because of the general decline in the coverage of trade unionism charted in the following chapter, or because the restructuring of work is featuring more prominently than before in traditionally non-union sectors, notably in areas of the private service sector.
2. The apparent reduction, within unionised establishments, of union influence over the way in which extra flexibility is brought in.
3. There does seem to be a qualitative difference between the basis on which much of the new flexibility has been introduced and the earlier tranche of changes associated with productivity

bargaining. The most striking difference is the extent to which the new changes represent genuine increases in managerial authority to deploy labour in patterns and on terms which they deem appropriate to production requirements, rather than a new rulebook changing the terms of the regulated effort/reward bargain but not, fundamentally, the degree of regulation itself.

Quality

There are many ways of measuring the growing importance attached by organisations in all sectors to the issue of quality – largely in recognition of the centrality of quality as a competitive differentiator in world markets. Some of the key indicators of organisations' response include:

■ Institutional innovations, for example the use of quality circles, quality councils, process improvement groups and so on, all with a common concern to involve directly cross-sections of staff in the process of raising quality standards and tackling identified problems.
■ The adoption of quality 'systems', notably BS 5750, that prescribe various ways of organising workflows, management procedures, and lines of responsibility in order to qualify for recognition as a 'quality' organisation.
■ The adoption of an organisation-wide programme or philosophy aimed at instilling a culture of 'total quality management', of a customer-first mentality, at all levels.

Extensive energy has been expended by UK business organisations on each of these areas in recent years. Rather as was the case with flexibility, the sense here is that there is nothing which in itself is fundamentally incompatible with the continuing existence of a union-based industrial relations system.

Perhaps we should not be surprised by this when we consider the light shed on the subject by the Workplace Industrial Relations Survey. It shows a rapid rise in the number of establishments reporting the introduction of a quality circle between 1984 and 1990 – but that these bodies were still only found to have been introduced in some 2 per cent of workplaces (5 per cent in the manufacturing sector). Five per cent of establishments were also reported to have introduced briefing or training groups in parallel.[15]

If developments under the quality banner seem to sit reasonably comfortably with a sense of continuity on the industrial relations front, what is their significance for the wider argument about the extent to which a distinctly new approach to HRM is being developed? Ron Collard, writing in *Strategies for Human Resource Management* painted a clear picture of the possibilities opened up for the human resource function by the Total Quality (TQ) movement:[16]

> (The HR function) should have the expertise required to develop and implement means of influencing the behaviour and attitudes of employees and to manage the cultural changes involved. TQ initiatives should be based on the research and analysis of present behaviours, attitudes, beliefs and competencies which lead to the design and organisation of education, training, communication, involvement and performance management programmes. All these are within the remit of the human resource function.

That said, there is no mistaking the scent of disillusion that wafts over much of the TQ scene. Notwithstanding the unmistakable evidence that a number of important businesses have in effect transformed themselves using, at least in part, concepts drawn from the TQ lexicon, and accepting also that quality and customer service precepts have helped provide crucial organising principles in new or drastically remodelled businesses (central government agencies spring to mind as examples), there does indeed appear to be ground for such cynicism. The charge is that, whatever its potential for helping establish a radically changed basis for 'the way we do things around here', total quality has too often been characterised by:

■ A concentration on the ephemeral trappings of a glossy programme, rather than changes of substance in methods of working.
■ An absence of tangible gains following early and extravagant promises.
■ The creation of a whole new bureaucracy of quality processes , rules and procedures.
■ 'Sheepdip' training carried out on a wide scale but with little or no link in to the jobs that the recipients will be going back to, and as a substitute for a real programme of culture change.

Commitment

Turning now to the third distinguishing feature of HRM – the drive to strengthen employees' sense of commitment to the enterprise – we find again that the Workplace Industrial Relations Survey[17] has some valuable data on recent trends.

- Newly-introduced arrangements for employee involvement were reported in 45 per cent of all establishments in 1990. This comes on top of a finding of 35 per cent in 1984.
- This activity was found in all parts of the economy but was particularly prevalent in the private services sector.
- There was a particular emphasis on relatively informal – or at least 'non-structural' innovations such as joint meetings, job satisfaction initiatives, team briefing, team working etc, rather than the use of formally constituted committees.

There is something of an overlap here between the drive to strengthen employee commitment and programmes such as TQ or customer service. Often the latter will be introduced as part of a 'culture change' programme which has as its dual objectives winning acceptance – enthusiasm even – for a set of changes in ways of working and a more thoroughgoing attitude shift and a reorientation towards the organisation's values. There are some spectacular and oft-quoted examples of organisations that have made a major effort to gain employee commitment to significant business changes. BA's 'Customer First' initiative, Ford's Employee Involvement project and Xerox's Total Quality programme are cases in point. Each exhibited, among other things, a significant investment in communication at all levels of the organisation.

In many ways the discussion of 'commitment' takes us to the heartland of what might be seen as the non-British model of HRM – the approach with the most transatlantic resonance and strongest unitarist thread running through it. The classic exemplar of this style is IBM. Writing in 1986, Philip Bassett[18] had this to say about the Big Blue's attitude to its employees:

> The company and its employees are characterised by a combination of individualist entrepreneurship within an overall corporate philosophy – and it is, crucially, a proselytising philosophy, too: IBM knows it has a message, a better way of doing things.

Interestingly, the recession of the early 1990s has put a new angle on this discussion. Typically the organisations which were most often cited as placing a high value on employee commitment were also seen as going to great lengths to offer their employees, as part of the psychological and cultural bargain, exceptionally high levels of employment security and higher than average terms and conditions. Indeed it was precisely this combination of high material rewards and security and strong individual attachment to the organisation that was deemed to be such bad news for trade unions, causing Guest[19] to argue that: 'If the four central components of HRM outlined earlier are considered, then ... the main challenge to the unions is likely to come from the pursuit of employee commitment.'

Yet one of the distinctive characteristics of the recent recession is that it has borne down heavily on some of the companies, and indeed sectors, most visibly identified with the high security/ high commitment approach. The announcement by IBM in 1990 for the first time, of significant redundancies, followed by an across the board pay standstill, followed by even more widespread redundancies in 1992, represented a most spectacular break with a strong, espoused corporate culture. It was accompanied by similar and commensurate changes in other parts of the IT industry (Hewlett Packard for example) and in other organisations whose strong emphasis on their commitment to their employees collided with the state of their order books (Marks and Spencer's unprecedented decision to declare redundancies among its management trainees was a clear case in point).

The point here is that the emphasis on 'employee commitment' as a defining feature of the 'new' HRM school draws heavily on what we saw described above as the 'soft' version of HRM, whereas the reaction of organisations to a steep recession shows the strong representation within those organisations of the 'hard' version, with its stress on cost, control and calculation. The difficulty and confusion arise when the organisations themselves have described their philosophies and policies to their staff in terms of the soft version, ('our people are our greatest asset' is of course the best-worn phrase in this regard), but then respond to events very much in line with the hard version – not least by laying off large numbers of those 'greatest assets' at short notice.

Strategic integration

This is the fourth and final of the defining features of 'new look' HRM. It is also the heading in which we find at its weakest the idea that there has been a systematic replacement of traditional approaches to managing workplace relations by a fully integrated and widely practised, more 'strategic' HRM.

Finding measures for the pursuit of strategically integrated HRM is not straightforward. We are talking about a fairly well-hidden phenomenon: one that revolves around the way in which organisations undertake key business processes and plan and deploy resources, and also about the power and influence enjoyed by different groups and levels of management over those processes.

A sensible starting point seems to be the position of the HR or personnel function itself. What evidence can we find on the extent to which the function is growing or declining in corporate significance?

Writing in 1988, Karen Legge[20] concluded that, taking the range of survey data then available, there were signs of an increased importance being attached to the personnel function within firms – and not just by personnel managers. There was also evidence of 'arguably, a small increase in areas of decision-making where, traditionally, personnel considerations have not loomed large'. Decisions on fixed capital investment, and major changes in production methods – although not, interestingly, the introduction of new technology – were cited as examples of increasing personnel involvement. The 1990 Workplace Survey seems to support this picture.

Another way of shedding light on the issue is to look at the representation of the HR function at the top of the organisation. Here the evidence seems to point the other way. The 1990 Workplace Survey finds a fall in board level representation for HR.[21] This finding needs to be taken together with Garnet Twigg and Philip Albon's observation in *Strategies for Human Resource Management*:[22]

> We have all met the 'marketing CEO' who is strong on product mix and marketing strategy, the 'financial CEO' strong on financial disciplines and processes, or the 'manufacturing CEO' strong on technology and systems. But do we know a 'HRD CEO' who is strong on gaining competitive advantage by developing his or her people?

Perhaps, however, we are looking through the wrong end of the telescope. Perhaps the extent to which a company practises integrated HRM is not to be measured in terms of the influence of the HR function but by the extent to which human resource considerations are taken up by non-specialist managers in the rest of the organisation.

The argument here is that where a personnel director is found on a main board but without a corporate personnel department, the organisation is likely to accord personnel considerations greater weight in decision-making than those with large functional departments, and to integrate those considerations into strategic decision-making in a manner consistent with HRM philosophy.

With this in mind it may be relevant that the 1990 Workplace Survey reports an overall increase in the time spent on HR issues by non-specialist managers, and indeed an increase in the number of such managers becoming involved in HR issues. This is not of itself, however, evidence for widespread integration on the part of HRM – certainly not in the strategic sense described above of incorporating human resource considerations into the process of corporate strategy.

Arguably this may in any event be to expect too much. The live issue may very well be 'who owns human resource management in the organisation?', and not 'how does human resource management fit in?', especially given the predominately piecemeal manner in which the vast majority of HRM initiatives have been introduced in recent years.

DRAWING THE THREADS TOGETHER

What are we to make of the results of this evidence? We set out to see how far we could track down in practice the existence of the differentiating features which the theory tells us would indicate the widespread adoption of HRM as a systematic *replacement* for more conventional approaches – especially for those which incorporate union-based industrial relations.

Two conclusions stand out. First, it is not possible to substantiate a case for such a systematic change. There are far too many indicators of continuity and of piecemeal change, of 'business as usual' on the part of central HR functions, on the one hand, and of opportunistic moves to introduce local changes in an *ad hoc* fashion on the other, to bear out such claims for root and branch transformation.

Reviewing the light that the 1990 Workplace Industrial Relations Survey could shed on the evidence for the existence of employee relations practices that were indicative of the adoption of HRM as an alternative blueprint, Neil Millward[23] has written:

'Broadly speaking, we could find little evidence that the very substantial growth in non-unionism was accompanied by a growth in HRM or more "progressive" management practices.'

Indeed a key conclusion of this research is that where 'fragments of HRM' were found they were as commonly or more commonly found in workplaces with recognised trade unions, not those without them, (although this begs the question of whether this might reflect employers using HRM techniques in order to bypass recognised trade unions – through, for example, the introduction of performance appraisal and performance related pay).

And yet, to come to the second point, to stop there would risk missing the point on an epic scale by concentrating too much on academic models and on the search for the pure example. For there is a clear sense running through this analysis that *something* has changed, and that the change is significant – even if it cannot be as neatly and instantly categorised as the models demand. A recurring theme is that to understand the nature of the change it makes sense to start with the 'who' rather than the 'what' questions.

- Who, typically within organisations, is taking the decisions that are ushering in new forms of working and new types of relationship?
- On what disciplines do they draw?
- What imagery do they employ in describing the process of change?
- Which communities do they feel part of?
- What do they regard as the legitimate forms of employee reaction to their own agendas?

Earlier in this chapter we noted Fowler's percipient comment that 'HRM represents the discovery of personnel management by Chief Executives'. We can go further than this, however. All the indications from the foregoing are that in many organisations, spread across all sectors, the initiative, in what previously would have been seen as the traditional area of concern of personnel management, has passed across to what we might term general or line management, at a variety of different levels. Moreover, in the process of this move something of a redefinition of that area has taken place, to the extent that what the line management community conceives of as 'people issues' differs in some important respects from the more constitutional and essentially pluralist agenda of personnel management and of industrial relations.

Organisational, market and technological change has been, and continues to be, the driver for much of this development. Well over half of the establishments covered by the Workplace Industrial Relations Survey in 1990 reported that they had experienced a major organisational/technological change during the course of the preceding four years. The prevailing pattern throughout this period has been for such change to fall into the province of chief executives, finance directors and information systems directors: certainly they are the ones who typically have the accountability and the influence *across* the organisation to drive through such programmes of change.

A number of observations can be made about this community of 'change agents':

■ This community has a conception of 'people issues' that draws almost exclusively from the 'hard' version of HRM. It is concerned with issues of cost control, the 'fit' of individuals to new systems and structures, and the extent of any immediate skill mismatches.

■ It tends to have a 'project management' approach to the management of change, in which the change process is conceived as a series of tasks, to be arrayed in a logical order and with mechanisms in place to monitor the implementation of the plan.

■ There is no real concept of the validity of a 'change by agreement' philosophy – or indeed of the essential legitimacy of a pluralist approach. Trade unions and other institutions of workplace regulation are at best a confounded nuisance to be bypassed, at worst an 'enemy within' to be vanquished.

John Storey, in his fascinating investigation[24] into the way in which management teams in a range of major UK businesses have reshaped working practices and workplace relationships, makes the following observation about this community:

> To a considerable extent the wave of change which swept many along in the eighties occurred as part of a wide process of diffusion. Ideas were carried from one organisation to another via conferences, consultants, the financial press, inter-company collaboration and so on. Hence, part of the language and lore of managers underwent a change. Certain commonalities began to emerge. Line managers, operational and staff managers from a range of functional specialisms became quite content to talk freely of their organisations needing further 'culture change'. The necessity for line managers to 'own' solutions to organisational problems was widely discussed. Training and development programmes for managers in areas such

as total quality gave further impetus to the spread of such ideas. For example, it is notable that the seminars run by Tom Peters ... are marketed as tools to give the edge to quality managers, line managers and sales and marketing specialists, but the levers to be pulled to effect the recommended changes are primarily ones in the people-management arena.

Storey[25] analysed the activities of 15 organisations introducing major programmes of change in recent years and found the following features to be common:

■ General/business/line managers to the fore.
■ Increased flow of communication.
■ Direct communication.
■ Prime guide to action: 'business need'.
■ Selection integrated.
■ Wide-ranging cultural, structural and personnel strategies.
■ Values/mission.
■ Customer orientation to the fore.
■ Teamworking.
■ Conflict reduction through culture change.
■ Aim to go beyond contract.

Taken together this list seems to represent a robust summary of what the 'new' HRM means in practice. It is connected, with varying degrees of closeness, to statements of corporate mission and values. It exhibits some important elements of internal integration of individual HR policies. It has a strong customer service ethos which is tied in with a stress on the promotion of teamworking. Line managers are seen as the driving force within it and they are both the conduits for, and are supported by, increased flows of communication to employees.

Before leaving this account there are two important qualifications to be made. The first is that the picture presented above draws very much from organisations that have made conscious and concerted efforts to *change* the way in which they run their businesses. This seems valid at a time of rapid business change and in a period also during which managers have become more accustomed to looking beyond the confines of their own organisations for examples of workable solutions which might be relevant to them. We need to remember, however, the wide swathes of the economy which have not undertaken such changes, or have simply picked up on one or two unintegrated aspects.

The second qualification is that these conclusions do not of

themselves answer one of the major questions which we posed at
the outset: is the development of HRM, in the broad shape that it is
taking in practice in the UK, necessarily at odds with the continued
existence of trade unions and other features of the traditional
industrial relations system? We have seen a number of features
(like the greater emphasis on direct communication with employees) which make life more difficult for trade unions, but none
which automatically make the disestablishment of trade unions a
management imperative. Indeed, for example, John Storey's 15
companies included many that negotiated, or at least consulted,
with trade unions over the introduction of change. He comments
that 'broadly speaking ... this period of innovation was not
accompanied by a frontal attack on the trade unions'; although he
goes on to note that 'in the main, trade union leaders both at
national and workplace level were left on the sidelines of most of
the managerial initiatives during this period'.[26]

This ties in with the fact that we have seen a much greater degree
of influence over these questions pass to a management community
whose values, outlook and attitudes might be expected to make
them more impatient of established workplace structures, less
inclined to see a positive role for trade unions in decision making
and, in particular, unlikely to see a business case for recognising
trade unions in new workplaces, or for bringing them in where
previously they have not been involved.

With this in mind we move on, in the next chapter, to look at
what has been happening to the machinery and procedures of
decision-making and representation within the workplace.

References

1. Hanson, C (1991) *Taming the Trade Unions*, Macmillan, London,
   pp xv–xvi
2. Storey, J (1992) *Developments in the Management of Human
   Resources*, Blackwell, Oxford, p 33
3. Ibid. pp 24–5
4. Ibid. p 26
5. Armstrong, M ed (1992) *Strategies for Human Resource Management*, Kogan Page, London, p 18
6. Legge, K (1989) 'Human resource management: a critical analysis',
   in Storey, J ed, *New Perspectives in Human Resource Management*,
   Routledge, London, p 26
7. Fowler, A (1987) 'When chief executives discover HRM', *Personnel
   Management*, 19 p 48

8. Storey, J *op. cit.* p 9
9. Guest, D (1989) 'Human resource management: its implications for industrial relations and trade unions', in Storey, J ed *op. cit.* p 43
10. Ibid. p 44
11. Ibid. p 42
12. Millward, N, Stevens, M, Smart, D and Hawes, W R (1992) *Workplace Industrial Relations in Transition, The ED/ESRC/PSI/ ACAS Surveys*, Dartmouth Publishing Company Ltd, Aldershot
13. Ibid.
14. Incomes Data Services, (1990) *IDS Study no 454*, IDS, London, March
15. Millward, N *et al op. cit.* p 178
16. Collard, R in Armstrong, M ed, *op. cit.* p 171
17. Millward, N *et al op. cit.* pp 166–70
18. Bassett, P (1986) *Strike Free*, Macmillan, London
19. Guest, D *op. cit.* p 43
20. Legge, K (1988) 'Personnel management in recession and recovery: a comparative analysis of what the surveys say,' *Personnel Review*, vol 17, no 2, p 62
21. Millward, N *et al op. cit.* p 49
22. Twigg, G and Albon, P in Armstrong, M ed, *op. cit.* p 86
23. Millward, N (1994) *The New Industrial Relations?*, Policy Studies Institute, London, p 130
24. Storey, J *op.cit.* p 121
25. Ibid. pp 82–3
26. Ibid. p 248

CHAPTER 5

Whatever Happened to Industrial Relations?

INTRODUCTION

'Industrial relations', the finance director wrinkled his nose in some distaste, 'didn't Maggie do away with all that nonsense?' Crude and over-simplistic though such an attitude may be, it is a reasonable approximation to a prevailing view among a large proportion of UK managers.

The phrase 'industrial relations' seems fated to remain tainted and burdened down with some highly prejudicial images and associations. Some iron entered the soul of British management at the end of the 1970s and its force is regularly refreshed by pieces of 'step-by-step' legislation, by the conversational reliving – in ever-more black and white terms – of past battles, and, every few years, by election broadcasts that give pride of place to increasingly grainy film footage of picket lines and piled-high uncollected rubbish bags.

The world of industrial relations, on this reading, is a bleak place. It is populated by over-mighty trade union 'barons' who, when they are not popping into 10 Downing Street for beer and sandwiches, are instructing union members to strike, picket and generally behave in an uncivilised fashion, and by surly and uncooperative shop stewards whose role in life is to say 'no' to any management proposal for modernisation (or indeed to anything else for that matter) and who thereby 'prevent managers from managing'.

This is a potent cocktail comprised of direct experience, selective rewriting of history, ideology and mythology. It has both fed and been fed by the strongest and most consistent theme of government policy, pursued without respite for 14 years by a self-confidently pro-enterprise and anti-union administration. Since 1979 eight major pieces of industrial relations legislation have been carried and these, together with a score or more of supporting actions and measures, have more or less completely rewritten the entire industrial relations rulebook. Throughout this whole process successive government ministers have been able to claim, with vocal support from the business community, that they have been cutting with the grain of modern managerial practice. The project has been presented as one that supports the process of moving away from reactive, fire-fighting and conflict-ridden crisis management, towards proactive, leadership-based and business-driven management of human resources.

In view of the scale of this project – and taking into account developments in human resource management thinking and in the ownership of HRM issues within the management community – the casual observer might expect to find a complete transformation of the landscape of workplace relations and the virtual extinction of the machinery and procedures associated with the 'outdated' mode of industrial relations.

In this chapter we shall be examining the extent to which such a transformation has taken place. There are a number of facets to this examination. One is legislative. Just how fundamental are the changes to the conduct of employee relations that have been ushered in by means of the successive rounds of legislation? What is the new balance sheet of rights and responsibilities affecting, respectively, employers, employees and their representatives: what actions and behaviours are now ruled out, what are still allowed? How does the European dimension fit in with this analysis? How important is the legislation – actual and draft – emanating from the European Commission in Brussels? What force might the 'Social Chapter' have in the UK after Maastricht and subsequent upheavals? How far does the new legislative framework actually cut with the grain and support what employers – for all the business-based reasons described in earlier chapters – actually want to do in practice?

Another facet is institutional. What is left of the institutional machinery of industrial relations? What has happened to trade union membership and to the recognition of trade unions? How are employers organised to conduct their workplace relationships? What about the third parties: the bodies concerned with adjudicating, regulating, mediating and arbitrating? We look at the industrial relations scene both through the traditional lens of the characteristics of the collectively organised sector and from the point of view of the non-unionised sector – especially of the erstwhile unionised but now de-unionised sector. Along the way we also take in the so-called 'new industrial relations' – the realm of the single union deal and the strike-free agreement.

Throughout this account we will be trying to understand the extent to which changes in the machinery and procedural structure of workplace relations are consistent with, indeed result from, the apparent shift in policy and paradigm charted in the previous chapters. Can we now say that UK employers have systematically replaced one model and system with another: that they have shed what we shall see described as the voluntarist/pluralist framework and adopted and institutionalised a unitarist/human resource management structure? Or shall we instead find a much more opportunistic, patchy and unthematic redrawing of the institutional landscape?

BACK TO THE FUTURE

The danger with an enterprise such as this is that we look at the recent past with the benefit of 20:20 rear vision. We reflect on the events of the 1970s and 1980s, in other words, through the eyes of the 1990s, and in so doing we invest recent history with an air of inevitability that is quite inappropriate to the passage of events, and which pays scant regard to the complexity of choice which existed at that time. In the case of what has been a contentious and fast-moving area such as industrial relations, the specific danger is that we will start off from the current paradigm of how things should be and portray the last fifteen or so years as a smooth progression from one failed model towards the 'new reality' of the 1990s.

We would, under such circumstances, merely accept without question the prevailing wisdom that industrial relations practitioners were entirely preoccupied with 'firefighting' – with the reactive 'must keep the show on the road despite the unions' outlook with which the industrial relations scene of the late 1970s is often characterised.

For this reason it seems appropriate to remind ourselves of some key aspects of the climate of the 1970s: to describe what it was that policy and practice have been reacting against during the subsequent two decades, and to disentangle myth from reality to some extent.

An influential text of the early 1970s, entitled *Management by Agreement*[1] argued that 'no area of management decision-taking is beyond the rightful concern of employees' and therefore that 'in terms of collective bargaining this means that any subject is a fit one for the negotiating table'. The underpinning argument for claims of this sort was that the power of workplace trade union representation had become so strong – and would inevitably and *legitimately* continue to grow in strength – that the only way of moving forward was to adopt a completely participative management style, to seek to incorporate trade union representatives into the pursuit of the corporate interest through joint regulation and power-sharing. This was the strategy described by Eric Batstone as 'giving up control in order to regain control'.[2]

That is the defensive formulation of the argument for 'management by agrement'. A more positive formulation was put – not surprisingly – by the government-sponsored report that in many ways marked the high point of officially-supported trade union aspiration: the 1977 Bullock report on Industrial Democracy.[3] The Bullock Committee proposed going far beyond the realm of extending the range of subjects covered by joint negotiation and on to the adoption of a *representative* approach – putting trade union representatives on to the boards of large companies in equal numbers to shareholder representatives. The argument for this radical change was couched in these terms:

> the problem of Britain as an industrialised nation is not a lack of native capacity in its working population so much as a failure to draw out their energies and skill to anything like their full potential. It is our belief that the way to release those energies, to provide greater satisfaction in the workplace and to assist in raising the level of productivity and efficiency in British industry – and with it the living standards of the nation – is not by recrimination or exhortation but by putting the relationship between capital and labour on to a new basis which will involve not just management but the whole workforce in sharing responsibility for the success and profitability of the enterprise. Such a change in the industrial outlook and atmosphere will only come about, however, as a result of giving the *representatives* of the employees a real, and not a sham or token, share in making the strategic decisions about the future of an enterprise which in the past have been reserved to management and the representatives of the shareholders.

It is fascinating to look back on such a passage now and find that it contains such strong echoes of the argument for the 'empowerment' of employees, which we saw in Chapter 3, being put forward by many management gurus as the only basis for building adaptive, flexible and competitive business organisations (although, crucially, the argument is for the empowerment of *representatives* rather than of individuals). This leads on to some other important distinctive features. One is a *political* argument that sees participation in management decision-making as intimately bound up with a broader societal change – away from deference and towards involvement, power-sharing and 'having a say' in all aspects of life.

The second distinctive feature is a very pluralistic concern with the structures of *power* in the enterprise. There is a sense of, in effect, suspicion that without the creation or institutionalisation of some structure of power which is independent of managements, the sharing, involving and empowering will not happen – or at least is unlikely to be sustained: left to their own devices managers will revert to a more autocratic type. This is a theme to which we will return in the next chapter.

This preoccupation with structures of power and with the need to find a more positive accommodation between the 'two sides' of industry is hardly surprising, given the terms in which 'the trade union question' was couched, and given also the central position which it had in public and policy debate. Running through that debate was a core assumption that the growth in trade union membership, representation and influence – which had been such a salient feature of the 1950s, 1960s and 1970s – was somehow inexorable.

The widely held consensus was that, like it or not, trade unions would continue to grow and would continue to spread their influence to more and more areas of national life. The issue therefore was how to channel that influence, how to come to terms with it and come to the most mutually satisfying (or perhaps the 'least-worst') arrangement or deal. And this brought into play the other core assumption, which was that a major problem was the weakness of trade union and industrial relations structures relative to the role that they had taken on for themselves or had thrust upon them. The concern then was not about the excessive *strength* of industrial relations institutions, but their relative *weakness*.

This had certainly been the principal line of argument of the Donovan Commission[4] on industrial relations in the mid 1960s. The Donovan analysis really underpinned the policy and practice of unions and employers alike and of governments of both persuasions for the subsequent decade and a half. The key points in this analysis were that:

- Within the unregulated and *ad hoc* system of British industrial relations, power had shifted towards the shopfloor: away from higher management and towards shop stewards and junior managers.
- As a result shop stewards had an excessive degree of influence over wages and work organisation that was detrimental to the enterprise and which, in aggregate, helped fuel the British economy's chronic tendency towards wage inflation.
- Therefore in the interests both of enterprise efficiency and of national economic policy, there was an urgent need to formalise, institutionalise and thereby control this informal industrial relations system.
- The answer lay in, on the one hand, formalising the procedures, rules and agreements governing workplace relations and taking control of bargaining out of the hands of lower levels of management and putting it into the hands of industrial relations specialists and, on the other hand, incorporating shop stewards into the formal structure of trade unions.

What this analysis did *not* challenge was the essentially 'voluntarist' approach that had characterised the regulation and legal underpinning of the British system of industrial relations. Indeed, it argued forcefully that collective bargaining was the most effective and the most democratic basis for conducting industrial relations and that the role of the law should be a very restricted one. The abstentionist tradition abjured labour 'codes', special courts, statutory rights, or the other features to be found in more interventionist legal systems (as were to be found in fact in almost every other country).

Instead, the law governing the conduct of industrial relations was based on a very British fudge. Common law had traditionally held no legitimate place for trade unions. In law the contract was held to be concluded between individuals and to be sacrosanct. Combinations of employees who banded together in order to exert pressure to change the terms of the contract – even to the extent of taking action to break the contract of employment – could only therefore appear in the eyes of the law as unlawful conspiracies against the public interest.

Since the contract of employment manifestly was not concluded between individuals of even standing and power but between an employer with economic power and employees without it, the law came slowly to recognise that the logical response was for employees to band together in order to try to equalise the balance of power in the contractual relationship. This recognition did not come by granting trade unions positive rights to do things such as organising or taking industrial action. Instead, unions, through a succession of individual judgements, were granted various 'immunities' from being sued for the breaches of common law that would inevitably arise from their activities. This approach survived for many years, being seen as broadly in line with the common-sense view of the nature of relations between employer and employee, and embracing also a pluralist notion of the 'balance of power' between employer and trade union. In broad terms the role of the law was to keep out of industrial relations: holding the ring and allowing the participants to reach voluntarily concluded deals.

THE CRACKS START APPEARING

By the end of the 1970s, however, this approach was under increasing strain, not least because under successive governments the area of industrial relations 'immune' from common law torts had first been restricted and then expanded very substantially. Also, there had been wild swings from the very legalistic approach of the Heath government's Industrial Relations Act through their u-turns and on to the 'partnership' and consensus-seeking approach of the Labour government's 'social contract'. There was also a strong and wide feeling that there had been significant abuse by unions of their newly-expanded immunities.

Underneath the political surface the degree of continuity and of adherence to the broad 'Donovan' pluralist consensus was considerable. Increasing numbers of workers joined trade unions. Employers recognised trade unions on an unprecedented scale and in respect of groups (such as managers) never before seen as part of the collectivist /pluralist system. They negotiated over an ever-wider range of issues – many of which had always previously fallen firmly within the realm of 'management prerogative'. They formalised their industrial relations in the ways recommended by the Donovan report – signing detailed procedural agreements, giving extensive facilities to full-time shop stewards and creating well-staffed, professional industrial relations departments. And they, and their associations and confederations, played a full and active part in the many and varied committees, commissions and councils that marked the tripartite industrial strategy pursued by the government of the day.

Many managers grew increasingly frustrated and irked by the growing list of industrial relations considerations that intruded into areas from which they had always hitherto been absent. They also came to believe that the balance of rights and responsibilities was being shifted unfairly against them.

They found it irksome and unfair, for example, that a company could be legally forced to recognise a trade union; that its wage levels could legally be set by an 'industrial court' on the basis of the 'going rate' for similar work in the same district; or that because of a contract that it had with a government department it could be forced to abide by the terms of a collective agreement to which it was not party and of which it had probably never heard.

They were frustrated by the constant tussles between unions and government over incomes policies and, indeed, by the constraints which incomes policies placed upon their company's freedom to employ the kind of workforce that they needed on the terms that were appropriate (although in overwhelming numbers they agreed that incomes policies were in principle 'a good thing' and in the national economic interest). In just the same way they expressed their distaste, outrage even, at the highly publicised industrial disputes which ran from the miners' strikes of the early 1970s through the seemingly constant background noise of trouble in the car industry, transport and Fleet Street, and of course culminating in the wave of industrial action in the 'winter of discontent' of 1978–9 which marked the collapse of the then government's pay policy.

To a large extent, however, they associated this with the poor state of industrial relations outside 'their' companies, just as trade unionists typically condemned strikes but thought that they were something done by unions other than their own. Alternatively, the poor state of industrial relations within companies was recognised by line managers and, indeed industrial relations specialists, but they felt inhibited from tackling it because of reluctance from the top of the organisation.

Despite these sources of grievance and frustration, however, at the end of the 1970s the prevailing wisdom throughout the great bulk of the management community remained broadly tolerant – even supportive – of the existence (if not the behaviour) of trade unions, seeing them as having a legitimate role in industrial life, and understanding of the attempts by the political and industrial establishment to incorporate trade union officials and representatives into areas of decision-making in order to encourage them to behave 'responsibly'.

It was therefore not in the industrial sphere but in the realm of politics that the revulsion against the pluralist/voluntarist consensus, which was to become such a dominant force in the 1980s, originated. Indeed, long after the election of a government pledged to 'take on' and 'sort out' the trade unions, many employers continued (and some continue to this day) to play by the old rules. In 1982, for example, the employers' national body, the CBI, was still sufficiently open to the concept of 'change by agreement' that it came within a whisker of signing a 'framework agreement' with the Trades Union Congress which recommended all employers to bargain over the introduction of new technology into the workplace, and to formalise their negotiations in the form of New Technology Agreements.

The strength of the political reaction against the then prevailing standards of industrial relations was crystallised in the scale of the swing, in the 1979 election, *against* a government which put the maintenance of good relations with trade unions at the top of its list of priorities and *towards* a party that was explicitly anti-union and vocal in its determination to break the industrial relations consensus. And, crucially, the votes of trade unionists, turning towards the Conservative Party in large numbers, contributed to a result that allowed the consensus to be broken. This was not to be a government that wanted to adjust the balance between employers and unions, it was to be one that simply had no patience with the very concept of a balance. As Sid Kessler and Fred Bayliss (two very experienced industrial relations practitioners) have written:[5]

> The government took pride in its convictions; pragmatism, fudging and nudging were what it rejected. But industrial relations is about bargaining between organised groups. The successful achievement of compromises, where the parties at first take their stands some distance apart, is the hallmark of its quality; back-up systems of conciliation and arbitration, often provided by government, are there to make good the failures of negotiators, not to inject new standards. As a method of regulating divergent interests in the workplace, industrial relations were based on a principle – that compromise is superior to conflict – which was the opposite of that adopted by the government – the market rules. The government was bound, therefore, to attempt major reforms in industrial relations...

But the government was not going to leave the future of the unions in the hands of employers. It set out to make a direct impact on the unions through legislation affecting both their internal government and their bargaining options.

STEP-BY-STEP-BY-STEP-BY-STEP

Looking back now on a decade and more of regular and radical industrial relations legislation, one is struck afresh by the constancy of purpose applied to this field by successive government ministers and officials. Not only was there no u-turn in the way that had originally been confidently predicted, no reversion to a search for consensus or the re-establishment of civil relations with the trade union movement, albeit on a much restricted basis. There has, if anything, been a ratcheting up of the legislative campaign: a determination at each stage of the step-by-step process to push the exercise even further next time.

Indeed, from the government's point of view, the beauty of the 'salami' approach to rewriting the industrial relations rulebook is that with each step a new benchmark is established, and the new reality is allowed to sink in for a couple of years, so that the next step then seems but a relatively short move on from the new benchmark. In this way moves that would have been seen as impossibly revolutionary at the outset of the programme (the legislation to interfere with the deduction of union subscriptions at source by employers – the 'check off' – and the removal of the force behind the TUC's 'Bridlington' rules on inter-union recruitment rights are the two latest examples) come to be seen as merely the logical next and small step along the road, and certainly nothing to get excited about!

Yet when we take the full range of legislative measures together we can see just how thoroughgoing the changes have been. The key features of the eight major pieces of legislation can be summarised as follows:

Employment Act 1980

■ Legal immunity for 'secondary' picketing (ie not at the employee's own workplace) removed in almost all cases.
■ Introduction of a 'conscience clause' protecting workers who refuse to join a union in a closed shop from dismissal.

- Requirement for a ballot, and for 80 per cent of the workforce who vote to affirm, before a new closed shop can be established.
- Dilution of protection against unfair dismissal: two years service required before cases can be brought.
- Abolition of statutory support for trade union recognition and for enforcement of 'going rate' of wages.
- Provision of public funds to cover the costs to unions of conducting secret ballots on strikes or internal elections.

Employment Act 1982

- All existing closed shops to be approved by large majority in ballots every five years.
- Removal of immunity in cases of industrial action which were either 'secondary' (ie not with the direct employer) or not 'wholly or mainly' related to terms and conditions of employment.
- Trade unions as organisations to be made accountable (and therefore, for the first time since the early years of the century, liable to be sued) for secondary picketing or for industrial action that was either secondary or went beyond the new definition of 'wholly or mainly' related to terms and conditions or which was taken to impose trade union membership.

Trade Union Act 1984

- All union executive council members with voting rights (therefore including most general secretaries) to be elected every five years by secret ballot.
- Secret ballots to be required before any industrial action called, otherwise the union loses all immunity from litigation in respect of broken contracts.
- Secret ballots to be required to reaffirm the existence of trade union political funds – the chief vehicle through which unions provide financial support to the Labour Party.

Wages Act 1986

- Restricted the powers of the Wages Councils, set up in the early years of the century to establish a floor of minimum wages in the least regulated 'sweatshop' sectors of the economy.

Employment Act 1988

■ Gave union members (as well as employers) the right to take union to court in the event of unlawful industrial action, and to avoid disciplinary action in the event of their crossing a picket line, working during a dispute, or in other ways breaking 'the rules of the club'.

■ Set up Commissioner for the Rights of Trade Union Members to support individual union members in complaints against their unions.

■ Effectively outlawed the closed shop by removing all immunity from unions in respect of industrial action to enforce the closed shop, and making it always unfair to dismiss an employee for non-membership of a union.

Employment Act 1989

■ Removed restrictions on the employment of women and young people, eg the ban on women working underground in mines and on night work for young people.

■ Exempted small employers from some employment protection obligations, eg to provide particulars of disciplinary rules.

■ Lengthened qualifying period of service needed before employees entitled to written statement of reasons for dismissal.

■ Limited the duty on employers to give union representatives time off to perform their trade union activities.

■ Ended trade union involvement in the training system by abolishing the tripartite Training Commission and introducing employer-led Training and Enterprise Councils (TECs).

Employment Act 1990

■ Abolition of pre-entry closed shop by making it automatically unfair to refuse employment on grounds of non-membership of a union.

■ All secondary industrial action now outlawed.

■ Unions made liable for unofficial action: requirement that senior figure in the union repudiates in writing unofficial strikes organised, say, by union shop stewards.

■ Employer now permitted to dismiss selectively employees who take part in unofficial action, without being liable for unfair dismissal.

Trade Union Reform and Employment Rights Act (TURERA) 1993

■ Complete abolition of the Wages Councils
■ ACAS to lose its statutory duty to 'promote collective bargaining'
■ A requirement for periodic reaffirmation by ballot by trade union members of their agreement to have trade union subscriptions deducted at source by the employer and paid automatically on their behalf to the union: the 'check off', which covers 80–90 per cent of the memberships of the largest unions and helps vastly to secure their income.
■ A removal of the force behind the TUC's so-called Bridlington rules and the introduction, in effect, of a free market in trade union membership.

The TUC's rules created 'spheres of influence' agreements between unions, regulating the rights of individual unions to recruit or organise in particular industries or organisations. 'Poaching' of members has always been a profound offence in the TUC's book, punishable by the ultimate sanction of expulsion from Congress. The TUC's rules were defended on the grounds that they encouraged stability and order, that they protected existing agreements with employers from being undermined by recruitment campaigns on the part of 'outside' unions, and that they protected unions from the large costs involved in competitive recruitment. The principle argument against is that in an era of consumer choice it is anomalous to have arrangements that deny the individual the right to 'shop around' and join the union that most attracts them. The provisions of the 1993 Act give individuals the right not to be refused membership of a union because they were previously a member of another union or because of an arrangement with another union which gives it sole recruitment rights in the company or sector concerned, and enable them to enforce that right through an industrial tribunal.

Just as the check-off provision is likely to do great damage to the membership position of individual trade unions, so the choice-of-union provision is likely to detract significantly from the authority and standing of the TUC, which derives in large measure from its ability to speak as the orchestrator and regulator of the combined trade union movement.

To complete this account of the government's rewriting of the industrial relations rulebook it is also important to have in mind both their actions as direct employers (the removal of trade union rights at GCHQ, for example, or their use of contracting out of public services in part to remove numbers of employees from the ambit of strong collective agreements) and also the systematic and determined drive to remove trade union nominees and representatives from public bodies, local and national committees and areas of public life, such as the training system, where previous administrations had sought their presence. The consistent theme has been to hammer home the view that the rightful role of trade unions is restricted to basic, local, 'bread and butter' issues and that their rightful place is not at the high table but in the equivalent of the boiler room.

DRAWING UP THE BALANCE SHEET

In summarising the combined impact of these measures on the industrial relations balance sheet, a number of key points stand out. First, the break with the voluntarist or 'abstentionist' tradition is absolute – and almost certainly irreversible. The conduct of industrial relations is now tightly regulated by legislative requirements, the institutions even more so: indeed there is a case for saying that trade unions, once widely considered to be 'above the law', are now subjected to more direct and intrusive legal regulation than any other institutions in British economic, civic or social life.

Employers have, moreover, gradually adjusted their behaviour in order to take advantage of the leverage that the new legislative framework gives them. The use of injunctions, for example, has become part of the tactical armoury of employers to influence the course of disputes, (hopefully to preempt them altogether), rather than to engage in acts of retribution against unions.

Although it is the changes in collective labour law that have proved most potent and eye-catching in their impact, it is important not to lose sight of the way in which changes in individual contract law have interacted with the main Employment Acts and have reinforced their efficacy. Not surprisingly, against this background, the role of lawyers has grown in line with the insertion of the law into industrial relations. The 1990 Workplace Industrial Relations Survey finds that the use by managers of legal advisors doubled during the preceding decade.[6]

The second observation is that, from the government's point of view, their programme has worked: the behaviour of trade unions and the balance of power between them and employers has shifted decisively. This result has confounded a widely-held previous view that the law would simply prove ineffectual in changing trade union practices. The force of the new arrangements and the accuracy of their design has been shown in a series of set-piece encounters which unions have entered into and from which they have almost consistently emerged as losers, with the power of the new rules firmly established at the end of these encounters with permanent force.

Thus for example the reality of the restrictions on secondary industrial action was brought home vividly in 1984 when the NGA print union attempted to prevent Eddie Shah's *Messenger* newspaper from using non-union labour by pressurising advertisers not to take space in the papers and journalists not to provide copy. The escalation of the dispute when the NGA ignored High Court injunctions and stepped up secondary picketing led to the sequestration of the NGA's assets, secondary industrial action by NGA members in the national newspaper industry and, in turn, a fresh round of injunctions and a decision of the Finance and General Purposes Committee (F&GPC) of the TUC to support secondary action in the industry. The personal intervention of TUC General Secretary, Len Murray, alone defused this potentially explosive situation, overruling the F&GPC and allowing the full General Council of the TUC to, in effect, recognise publicly for the first time that the legal changes were real and had to be respected, however detested they were.

The print industry also witnessed other demonstrations of the potency of the new laws, most noticeably in the clandestine move of Rupert Murdoch's News International papers to Wapping. This was accompanied by the complete dismissal of all members of the workforce who struck in protest, and their replacement with non-union labour (using common law rather than the new legislation), a successful use of injunctions to stop secondary action and defeat secondary picketing, and again the sequestration of the unions' assets. The success of the new limits on picketing (when enforced through very muscular policing) was shown most spectacularly during the year-long miners' strike in 1984. The 1989 abolition of the Dock Labour Scheme demonstrated the impotence of one of the most tightly and defensively well-organised groups of trade unionists to protect their position against a simple piece of legislation that completely removed the regulations that had hitherto given them a unique degree of employment protection.

THE NEW INDUSTRIAL RELATIONS SETTLEMENT

One of the reasons that trade unions have found it so difficult to mount any effective campaign against the government's legislative programme is that the measures that have pressed in on them most severely and negatively as *organisations* have all been expressed in positive terms as rights to *individuals*, including those to individual trade union members. The strong strand of individualism woven through the government's approach, and its relationship to their overall economic policy, has been summed up in the following terms by Kessler and Bayliss:[7]

> On matters like the closed shop, picketing, and ballots before strikes, the key idea was that collective action and its restraints on individual choice should be made to give way to wider individual preferences on whether or not to join a trade union, or cross a picket line, or join a strike even if a majority had voted in favour of it. Legislative action of a detailed kind on these matters was based on the belief that if individuals could choose they would tend to reject collective action and the government's objective of reducing impediments to the working of the labour market would be served.

This sense that the onslaught on traditional forms and methods of industrial relations was somehow moving with the spirit of the times and was cutting with the grain of a more assertive society-wide individualism became stronger as the 1980s progressed and turned into the 1990s. Its culmination came in the eventual acceptance by the TUC and the Labour Party of the principal planks of the new system of industrial relations law and their realisation that earlier pledges to repeal the changes were deeply unpopular with the public – and indeed with trade union members.

The real measure of the extent of the shift from the post-war consensus, therefore, lay in the fact that by 1992, from the point of view of industrial relations law, the gap between the two main political parties at the general election had shrunk enormously. A

Labour government, had one been elected, would have left untouched virtually all of the 1980s legislation covering the redefinition of legal industrial action and picketing, the abolition of the closed shop and the conduct of trade union affairs, including all of the balloting provisions. It would have looked favourably at proposals to introduce some legislative support for trade union recognition, although it had no firm proposition ready to enact. It would have strengthened considerably the employment rights available to individual workers (in areas such as protection against unfair dismissal, parental leave entitlement, health and safety and so on) and would then have left it to unions to promote themselves as the effective enforcers of such new rights.

This reversal of the customary Labour approach – legally defining the standard of employment contract deemed appropriate, rather than using the law to strengthen the institutions of labour market intervention, but then leaving it to the actors to define through negotiation the terms of the employment contract – demonstrated the completeness of the break with the voluntarist tradition towards the regulation of industrial relations.

A Labour government would also have taken a very different attitude towards the intervention of the European Union in the definition of labour market standards. It would have signed Britain up to the Social Chapter of the Maastricht Treaty and thereby opened the way to some additional regulation in terms of the working environment, health and safety at work, equal opportunities in employment and working conditions. Nothing in the Social Chapter is at odds with the legislative changes concerning the conduct of employer–trade union relations, although a Labour government might have helped breathe some life into the efforts of the EU through a variety of devices to introduce a legally supported, EU-wide extension of information and consultation rights for workers and their representatives.

The re-election of a Conservative government in the UK in 1992 and the turmoil experienced post-Maastricht in the EU seems, for now, to have contained the pressure on Britain to follow a more pluralist, 'social partnership' approach towards employment affairs and industrial relations. This leaves us with a new legally-defined and judicially-enforced industrial relations system, many of whose key features are likely to endure any foreseeable political change domestic or European – over the next decade or so. And that new framework differs sharply from the previous model in the following key ways:

- An enormous restriction in the scope for unions to organise and take action within the law except in respect of 'bread and butter' issues with the immediate employer: secondary, 'solidarity' or political action has been effectively outlawed.
- Detailed legal intervention into the rules and procedures governing trade unions, including both their government and their industrial activities, which has simultaneously increased the legal rights of members against their unions and made it more difficult for unions to react decisively in response to employer actions.
- A significant reduction in the statutory rights to employment protection available to individuals against their employers in the name of 'freeing up' the labour market and lifting the burden from employers.

FREEDOM OF CHOICE FOR EMPLOYERS

We have been looking at the rewriting of the industrial relations rulebook in terms, largely, of what it now *prevents* trade unions, and trade unionists, from doing. To complete the account it is important to turn the prism and to focus on what the new rules of the game *allow* employers to do. The short answer, not surprisingly, is that it allows them a far wider degree of freedom than for decades in choosing the basis on which they will conduct their relationships with their employees, in deciding whether or not to recognise trade unions – and if so which one(s) – as part of their employee relations scene, and in determining the contractual terms and conditions of employment.

Professor Lord Wedderburn has described the underlying thrust of the 1980s legislation as 'the doctrine of enterprise confinement'.[8] This has meant that the only model of trade union operations recognised by the law is one that limits its concerns, representations and activities to the organisation, and indeed the specific workplace location, employing the trade unionists concerned. Arguments based on comparability with other organisations, or indeed other parts of the same organisation, have no legal place or underpinning; action taken in support of workers elsewhere is ruled out on the grounds that it is 'secondary', that which is taken on issues going beyond the specific contents of the employment contract is ruled out on the grounds that it is 'political'.

For employers who continue to recognise trade unions, therefore, the new framework of law aligns with and supports the movement, charted in earlier chapters, to decentralise and divisionalise business activity and to internalise their labour markets – creating patterns of work organisation, job definitions and contractual terms and conditions tailored to their specific needs, rather than importing them ready made from national collective agreements. It enables them to minimise the involvement of external trade union officials and the impact of national or sectoral union policies, dealing instead with 'their' people – local trade union representatives – who are employees of the organisation itself rather than of an 'outside' body.

For employers who choose not to deal with a trade union the law continues, as it always has, to underwrite that choice. If an organisation wishes to end the recognition of a union with whom it has previously dealt (a case study of one such organisation is included in Chapter 7), the way forward is now cleared of legislative obstacles, even to the point that the employer can now selectively dismiss strikers without fear of industrial tribunal action. If an organisation wishes to resist the pressure from a union for recognition where previously there has been none, the cards are now stacked heavily in the employer's favour. Many of the methods through which unions used to seek to enforce a claim for recognition – ACAS-sponsored workforce ballots, secondary industrial action against suppliers or customers (or the threat thereof), the use of the Fair Wages resolution, and so on – have been rendered either illegal or impotent.

One of the manifestations of this new era of enhanced employer choice which attracted considerable attention in the 1980s was the 'new realism' of the single union deal. Deals such as those reached at Nissan, Sanyo, Matsushita, and more recently at Toyota's new car plant, have largely been features of new 'greenfield' sites and very often have been pursued by inwardly-investing companies. The interest aroused by these agreements has been disproportionate to the number of employees actually covered by them which, on recent estimates, still may not be much more than 50,000 or so. However, the significance of these agreements lay not in their numerical coverage but in the radical terms in which they were couched, and thus in the way in which they highlighted the new freedom for employers to set down the rules of engagement.

The key elements of these deals have been:

■ Single union representation, with constraints put on the role of union full time officials.

- Flexible use of labour across traditional demarcation lines.
- Single status: harmonisation of conditions between manual and non-manual staff.
- Participation – usually by means of a company council.
- The resolution of disputes by means of devices such as pendulum arbitration, a commitment to continuity of production and a 'no strike' provision.

The other distinctive feature of these agreements is the extent to which they have been led by the employer rather than by the union. In a reversal of past practice unions are invited to present themselves in a competitive 'beauty contest' and to give an account of what they can contribute to the company's success – and to do so moreover, typically before the first employee is recruited.

THE NEW MAP OF INDUSTRIAL RELATIONS

We have seen how radically the industrial relations framework has been reshaped; we have also noted in particular the large-scale expansion in the freedom of employers to choose the basis on which they wish to conduct their employee relations. The key question therefore concerns the extent to which employers have exploited their new freedom. To what extent have employers set about re-arranging the furniture in a significant way and changing the institutional and procedural arrangements governing the conduct of their relationship with their employees? How far have they cut the ties with the structures that did *not* reflect their divisionalised and devolved basis of operations? To what degree have employers sought to make institutional space within which to practise the principles of strategic HRM: line management ownership, flexibility, connection to the business objectives and empowerment?

Until very recently it has been possible to put up a plausible 'not much' answer to all of these questions. Throughout the mid to late 1980s a series of surveys and research projects could be interpreted as giving the same basic message: that underneath the surface of the dramatic political and legal changes being pushed through by the government the everyday reality for practical people was, for the most part, one of 'business as usual'.

The principal components of this case consisted of the following empirically-justifiable propositions and observations:

- The fall in trade union membership, though widespread, was essentially a reflection of the way in which unemployment had grown in the economy and had been concentrated in industries, regions and trades marked by relatively high unionisation.

■ The use of the new legal framework by employers was essentially tactical – designed to add another string to their bow in cases of industrial dispute rather than to completely redefine employee relations structures.

■ With the exception of some spectacular and highly-publicised instances, the practice of de-recognising trade unions was almost unheard of; the redefinition of the grounds on which employers would deal with unions was more widespread but still encompassed the basics of terms and conditions.

In the light of more recently available data – and in particular the 1990 Workplace Industrial Relations Survey – the claim that there has been more continuity than radical change will no longer stand up. The map has changed; the change is a radical one, and looks set to be a lasting one.

Take first the level of trade union membership. In the mid-1980s it was still possible to argue that unions were shrinking as they always did in recessions, but that, just as before, they would grow again during the recovery phase. That did not happen. The key discontinuity occurred when union membership failed to recover as employment recovered in the Lawson boom of the late 1980s. This meant that the trade union movement went into the recession of the early 1990s on a declining trend and then lost ground even more rapidly.

The extent of that lost ground is best described not in terms of absolute numbers but in terms of *density*: the proportion of the employed labour force who belong to trade unions. Figure 5.1 shows how that proportion grew steadily through the 1960s and 1970s, peaked at the threshold of the 1980s and has fallen steadily since.

The evidence from the 1990 Workplace Survey shows how far this trend intensified in the late 1980s. By the end of the decade the density of union membership had fallen from 58 per cent in 1984 to 48 per cent in 1990. Moreover since the survey excludes workplaces with 25 employees or fewer the real figure is probably *below* 40 per cent and around 30 per cent in the private sector.

The survey also confirms the view that the derecognition of trade unions by employers has been quite widespread with, on one estimate, almost one in ten workplaces doing away with trade union recognition between 1984 and 1990. Some care is needed with this figure. It includes workplaces where unions disappeared

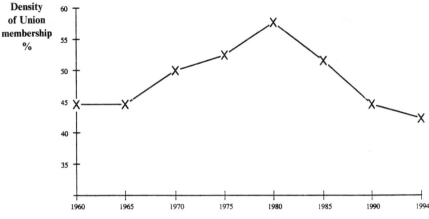

Figure 5.1 The rise and fall of unionisation

Source: Employment Department Gazette
Note: 'Density' of membership is total trade union membership as percentage of total employees in employment

not through conscious employer choice but because a small pocket of previous union members simply drifted away from the union. It also reflects a large group of employees – teachers – who, controversially, are deemed to have had their unions derecognised on the grounds that their pay is now determined by a government-appointed review body rather than by collective bargaining.

Nonetheless the evidence of a severe shrinking of the union-organised part of the labour market is clear and is reflected in the finding that the proportion of the working population whose pay is essentially determined by collective bargaining fell over the same period from 71 per cent to 54 per cent.[9] Again adjusting for workplace size, the true figure across the whole economy is closer to 40 per cent.

Figure 5.2 summarises the movement in the key dimensions of the institutional fabric of industrial relations across the three successive Workplace Surveys of 1980, 1984 and 1990.

CONCLUSIONS

The message is clear. In the early and mid-1980s the structure of the traditional 'industrial relations system' still held. By 1990 it did not. It is now wrong to depict the UK scene as one in which traditional, union-based industrial relations is the norm: such a

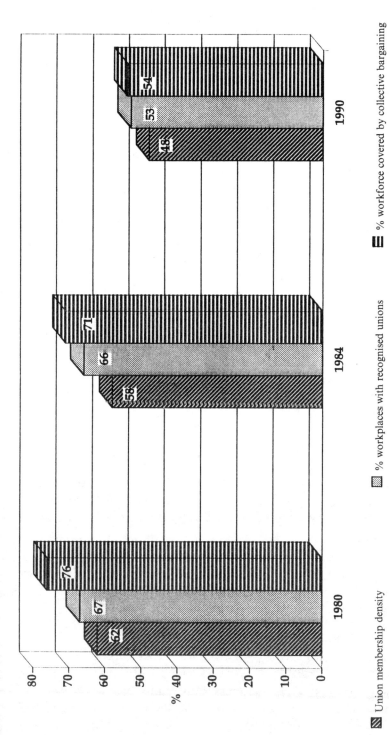

Figure 5.2 The industrial relations 'system' loses ground

Source: Workplace Industrial Relations Survey

system covers some, at most, 40 per cent of the economy. Parts of that sector are stable and their system is secure; other parts are either in long-term structural decline or, as in the public sector, face policy shifts such as market testing which are likely to reduce the degree of unionisation and collective bargaining.

The remaining 60 per cent of the workforce are employed in a different world that is non-unionised and not based on the practice of collective bargaining. Moreover this is the sector that is growing and which contains many of the more economically-dynamic business organisations.

In the next chapter we will focus on how the employment relationship is being conducted in these two sectors: what is the agenda of issues that employers and managers are seeking to pursue; to what extent does the agenda differ between the unionised and the non-unionised sectors; and to what extent does the way in which the issues are handled differ.

One concluding point is that the Workplace Industrial Relations Survey data shows some of the diversity of practice in the growing non-union sector. There are undoubtedly instances where organisations have pursued many aspects of the HRM paradigm described in earlier chapters. They are far from being the norm, however. Drawing on the Workplace Survey it is possible to put forward the following set of features that tend to distinguish the non-union sector from the more traditional unionised sector.

- Employees in the non-union sector are likely to receive much less information from their managers, and there are fewer channels for information and consultation than in the unionised sector.
- There are fewer health and safety representatives in the non-union private sector and the incidence of accidents and injuries is higher.
- Employees in this sector are two and a half times as likely to be dismissed as their unionised counterparts and the incidence of compulsory redundancies is higher.
- Labour turnover is higher in the non-unionised sector.
- There are no strikes in the non-unionised sector and fewer grievance and disciplinary procedures.
- The dispersion of pay is wider than in the unionised sector. It is more market related and there is more performance-related pay. There is also a greater incidence of low pay.
- A higher proportion of employees in this sector work on short-term or temporary contracts, work freelance, or in other ways

come within the sphere of 'peripheral' or 'precarious' employment.

■ There are fewer personnel specialists to be found in the non-union private sector.

■ Managers in this sector are more likely to feel that there is a 'better climate' in their organisation. They are also more likely to report that staff morale is lower.

Here then is a picture of considerable employer and managerial freedom and scope for choice. As the Director of the Workplace Survey has pointed out, however, the survey did not find that the growth of non-unionism was accompanied by the growth in HRM, or more 'progressive' management practices.[10] Some important questions are emerging about what employers are doing with their new-found freedom of choice, and also about the balance sheet of these choices in terms of efficiency and economic benefit. These are questions to which we shall return in the following chapters.

References

1. McCarthy, W and Ellis, N (1973) *Management by Agreement*, Hutchinson, London, p 97
2. Batstone, E (1988) *The Reform of Workplace Industrial Relations*, Clarendon Press, Oxford
3. *Report of the Committee of Inquiry on Industrial Relations*, (1977), HMSO, London, p 160, emphasis added
4. Royal Commission on Trade Unions and Employers' Associations (1968), HMSO, London
5. Kessler, S and Bayliss, F (1992) *Contemporary British Industrial Relations*, Macmillan, London, p 65
6. Millward, N, Stevens, M, Smart, D and Hawes, W R (1992) *Workplace Industrial Relations in Transition, The ED/ESRC/PSI/ ACAS Surveys*, Dartmouth Publishing Co Ltd, Aldershot, p 48
7. Kessler, S and Bayliss, F *op. cit.*, p 58
8. Wedderburn, Lord (1989) 'Freedom of association and philosophies of labour law', *Industrial Law Journal*, 18, p 28
9. Millward, N *et al op. cit.* p 92
10. Millward, N (1994) *The New Industrial Relations?*, Policy Studies Institute, London

CHAPTER 6

Employer Choice in Practice

INTRODUCTION

In the last chapter we looked at how the employee relations landscape has been radically reshaped in the last decade and a half. We saw the extent to which the long-entrenched and long-expanding 'British system' of industrial relations, with its collectivist structures, pluralistic ethos and its emphasis on the generation of rules governing both the procedural and substantive aspects of the employment relationship, had shrunk in importance: to the extent that it now arguably covers only around a third of the economy.

As a result of this transformation employers in the UK now have a greater degree of freedom than for many past decades in deciding how they structure and conduct their relationship with their employees – and arguably more than is the case in just about any other industrialised country.

The extra latitude and power given to employers extends to whether or not they decide to recognise a trade union to represent their workforce, whether or not to negotiate with them and whether or not to honour the terms of any agreement reached on their behalf. It covers, to an unprecedented degree, the wages and conditions that they decide to extend to staff, the basis on which they hire and fire them and the way in which they treat them once having employed them. By any standards this is a remarkable reweighting of the balance of power between employer and employee.

The purpose of this chapter is to throw some light on how employers have been using their new found freedom and power in practice:

■ What agenda of issues have they been pursuing?

- What consistent trends are there in the in the ways in which employers have been rewriting the *substance* of the employment contract?
- In what major ways have they been redesigning the *procedures* and *institutions* of employee relations?
- What is the emerging spectrum of mainstream choice within which the majority of employers are going to place themselves in deciding upon the basis for conducting their industrial relations?

From this analysis we go on to look at the extent to which the actions taken by employers in the field of employee relations, using their new-found freedoms, are consistent with what earlier chapters told us would be effective strategies for managing complex and large scale organisational and business change.

In this context we return to the question of unitarism versus pluralism as the basis for managing employee relations. We look at how, in practice, organisations can now quite feasibly organise and manage these relationships on a non-partnership, unitarist basis. Moreover we emphasise the precarious toehold that pluralist structures – that is, those that are based on the notion of an employees' interest that is *independent* from that of the employer – now have, even in areas of previous strength. Not least this is because of the collapse of an earlier prevailing view among many managers that supported, or at least did not actively resist, the presence of an independent trade union voice for their employees.

At the same time the chapter suggests that in some circumstances, whatever the degree of employer hostility, there is a 'public interest' case for the existence of an independent, pluralist employee voice. The difficult question that this leaves unanswered is whether this public interest can readily be reconciled with the perceived self-interest of employers in the 1990s and beyond in the way that it was in the middle decades of the twentieth century.

CHANGING THE AGENDA

Throughout the last decade employers have become, to a degree virtually without precedent, proactive in determining the agenda of issues shaping the employment relationship. It is true that in earlier chapters we could not depict a neat and comprehensive shift across the economy from one 'model' of employee relations to another: from pluralist industrial relations to unitarist, full-blown strategic

HRM. However, this emphatically does not mean that there has been more continuity than change in the employment relationship. As we shall see there has been a great deal of change and there are many common features in the ways in which organisations have set about reshaping their employee relations. Differences do, naturally enough, emerge: some of them related to the particular circumstances or cultures of specific sectors – or of broader delineations between, say, public and private sectors; some to the tactical judgements of local managers; many of them, crucially, related to the skills and abilities of managers to see through and sustain positive changes in the employment relationship.

This is an important part of the developing picture. In taking advantage of the greater scope for managerial freedom and employer choice, by being more proactive about driving change forward, organisations have, often unwittingly, been drawing attention to the capabilities of their managers – and in particular of their middle managers, into whose hands most of the tools and levers of change have been falling. Without making too much of this point it has to be said that this has not typically in the past been identified as a major source of strength in British organisations – especially when that middle management ability is applied to the management of people in large numbers.

What then is the agenda of issues that managers have been pursuing with their new powers and freedoms?

The first very clear point is that they have worked hard to change *working practices* – especially those previously protected by union strength. Reductions in the size of the workforce, changes in its composition and increased flexibility in the deployment of workers have been major features of the 'shake out' of the 1980s and the continuing push by employers, which has left unions almost continuously on the back foot.

■ The CBI's data bank of settlements showed that the working practices of three-quarters of manufacturing employees covered by agreements between unions and employers were altered during the 1980s.
■ More than half of all bargaining groups experienced more than one wage settlement involving changes in working practices.
■ Nearly a third of annual wage settlements throughout the decade included changes in working practices.

The evidence seems to support a picture of a general move towards enlarging the scope and responsibilities of jobs and the creation of a greater degree of overlap between them. This has been as much in response to organisational as to technological change. It has stemmed more from reductions in staffing levels, moves to reduce 'waiting time' and to increase effort levels across the working day as to any move to upskill the workforce or break down the continuing barriers that set apart production, maintenance and office jobs. A 1992 study, for example, confirmed that task flexibility had tended to increase the *breadth* of the range of the tasks undertaken by production and maintenance workers, but had not resulted in a *deepening* of skills.

The additional room for manoeuvre given to employers in determining workplace practices has tended to be used for a general cutback in the number of workers employed, a widening of individual job responsibilities and a tightening up of labour discipline. This has been pursued by way of unilateral management action much more frequently than in the past days of 'productivity bargaining'. This is all absolutely consistent with the model of 'hard HRM' described in Chapter 4, and indeed with the pursuit of an aggressive industrial relations style pursued in more conventional terms. There is much *less* evidence for the qualitative, functional job flexibility linked to a deepening of skills and a radical extension of responsibility and empowerment that would be the hallmark of the 'soft' version of HRM.

Other items on the management agenda, on the other hand, fit much more closely with the softer version. Concepts which have intruded with increasing prominence as the 1980s gave way to the 1990s include:

- Performance related pay.
- Performance appraisal.
- Training and staff development.
- Harmonisation of conditions.
- Teamworking.
- Communications.

Many of these – teamworking is a good example – have been pursued as part of a quality or flexibility initiative. Some (communications is the case in point) have had an overarching significance and have been pursued often as a 'good thing' in their own right. What they all have in common is a preoccupation with the management of *individual* relations with staff – indeed with the *individualisation of* employment relationships and policies in areas where they were previously handled on a more collective 'bulk purchase' basis. This comes out clearly when we recap on some of the main developments on these new agenda items.

The spread of *performance related pay* was one of the most striking changes introduced into the employment relationship over the last 15 years. Typically, the motivation for its introduction or renewal comprised some combination of a desire for more selectivity in the allocation of the paybill, a greater emphasis on accountability, a belief that individual motivation and thereby performance could be enhanced by linking pay to the achievement of pre-set objectives – and a dash of fashion-consciousness. An IPM/NEDO survey published in 1992[1] suggested that *two-thirds* of employers had individualised performance-related pay schemes for all or some of their staff. Twenty seven per cent of non-manual schemes had been introduced within the last ten years; 20 per cent within the last five years. Some five million employees – one-fifth of the workforce, are now covered by such arrangements.

Communications has been an area of fundamental change in the 1980s and 1990s. Managements have typically moved from a model of communications in which they are the respondents to demands for the disclosure of more information than they had initially intended to reveal, to communications programmes conceived and conducted as a way of setting the agenda and 'getting their message across'. This represents a very clear switch from a pluralist to a unitarist approach.

The renewed emphasis on communications has had a number of different aspects:

■ It has concentrated on establishing direct channels between the employer and the workforce – often on an individualistic basis – bypassing the previously established formal structures in which managements communicated indirectly with employees through union representatives. Where unions still exist they will tend to be treated as just one more constituency with information needs that carry no more priority than any other group.
■ The most consistently applied model has been the 'cascade' of information down through successive levels of the management chain, often in the form of team briefings in which managers give the line to 'their' people on the basis of a common rubric.
■ Organisations have been at pains to ensure that employees gain not only information that relates to their specific local circumstances but also to the 'big picture' of the business goals and circumstances of the organisation.

This account gives an indication of the benefits, but also the high potential cost, of trying to operate on a unitarist basis – compared to the alternative of communicating indirectly to employees through trade union channels. In the absence of these channels, a sustained and visible commitment to a consistently open communications policy is necessary: one that holds up in times of stress and which overcomes the natural inclination to believe that, since information is power, those in charge will tend to be economical with its dissemination.

The individualistic theme running through this agenda shows through quite strongly: the search for policies and approaches that define the employment relationship in much more personal and specific terms than those of a collective agreement. Performance appraisal is used to set individual objectives and to manage individual performance; training and development needs are expressed in individual training plans; and the organisation communicates directly with the individual employee.

The individualistic theme has affected the area of *pay* in a number of different ways. Many organisations have in effect removed their managers from the field of collectively-negotiated pay which, in the 1970s, had spread progressively up the occupational structure, by putting them on to individual contracts. This policy – used by BT for its managers, and by national newspapers for journalists and editorial staff – is sometimes accompanied by explicit derecognition of the relevant trade union; in other instances the union remains but, cut off from the pursuit of its central bargaining function, it may decline into irrelevance.

SEIZING THE INITIATIVE

When we review the changing landscape of employee relations we are struck by the extent to which employers have succeeded in taking the lead in deciding how that relationship is to be conducted – what channels, mechanisms, structures and processes are to be used, what issues are to be pursued and who will have the ability to influence that agenda. We saw some of the manifestations of that in the previous chapter: the discernible trend towards ending trade union recognition,the tightening up on the facilities provided by the employer to trade union representatives, the simplification of bargaining structures, evidenced by the spread of 'single table' arrangements in place of multiple bargaining units.

These, however, are all institutional, or procedural, changes. Of equal, if not even greater, significance is the fact that even where employers have not changed formal structures they have been able to behave with a much greater degree of freedom than would, in earlier years, have been imaginable, by redefining unilaterally how business can be conducted *within* these structures. This concentration on *content* rather than *structure* has been widespread.

The 1990 Workplace Industrial Relations Survey is, once again, a useful starting point for a review of this trend.[2] Comparing the findings for 1990 with those for 1980 and 1984, the survey finds that:

■ Within workplaces where unions continued to be recognised for collective bargaining, fewer employees were covered by the results of negotiations.

■ Fewer issues were subject to joint regulation between managements and unions in 1990 than in 1980. Managements were particularly successful at removing the question of employment levels and associated issues, such as redundancy and redeployment, from the bargaining table.

■ Equally, managements were successful at preventing trade unions from bringing issues to the bargaining table, such as the introduction of new technology, training and equal opportunities, which they identified as policy priorities but which managers saw as lying within the field of their own responsibility.

■ Beyond the area of formal negotiation, by the end of the 1980s union representatives were being consulted less often than before and being given less information than before on a number of issues. So some issues that had previously been the subject of formal joint national regulation were pushed down into the less binding area of local 'consultation'; other issues were simply taken out of the whole area of management–union discourse.

The major qualifications to this picture were that pay and the basic conditions of employment (such as hours of work) remained the primary focus of joint regulation in unionised environments, and that, secondly, in 1990 more establishments with recognised trade unions had formal disciplinary and dismissal procedures than at the start of the decade. Also, the tendency for managers to deal with disciplinary matters outside the agreed formal procedure was less apparent at the end of the decade than at the beginning.

So we can see a shrinkage in the area of joint regulation of employment not just because of the withdrawal of formal recognition from trade unions but also because of the redefinition by managements of what can be negotiated, what may be subject to consultation and what might be an issue for communication – and of the levels at which these will operate.

This conclusion holds in the public sector as well as the private sector, although there is a set of issues involved in public sector industrial relations that is distinctive, and without a clear 'read across' to private industry. The fact, for example, that local authority services are managed by/on behalf of elected representatives raises a different debate about the role of collective bargaining than the more straightforward issue of management 'prerogative'. Equally, the residual sentiment that public sector bodies should be 'good' employers tends to create a different agenda than one arising solely out of the distribution of profit.

Trade union organisation and the other formal features of the 'British system' are still significantly stronger in the public than in the private sector. Trade union recognition is much more widespread, the density of trade union membership is higher, the coverage of collective bargaining is more extensive, facilities for shop stewards are superior, and the incidence of strikes is more frequent. Moreover the large, hierarchically-organised and remotely-managed 'factory' workplaces (whether producing widgets or paperwork) which are the homeland of so many features of our traditional industrial relations are now very clearly a public sector rather than private sector phenomenon.

That said, we have already seen how far the government has moved to reduce the scope and size of the public sector through privatisation and contracting out – and how extensively they intend to build on this through the Next Steps agency programme, through compulsory competitive tendering of local authority services and through market testing in national government. These moves are affecting the structure of employment regulation. The substantive content too has been, and is being, restricted, in ways akin to the private sector, by management decisions to reduce the scope of what is bargained over and to resist union initiatives to bring new issues to the bargaining table.

This review fits with the conclusions drawn by John Storey from his analysis of developments in a series of 'mainstream' large companies:[3]

among the 15 (survey companies) there was only one where a clear, unambiguous policy intent to derecognise the main unions both existed and was admitted to. More common was a generally more aggressive stance towards the unions but without any apparent agenda (hidden or otherwise) to displace them. The companies took the fight to the unions who found themselves, for the first time in some while, simply responding to management's agenda of issues.

Storey goes on to make the very sound point that this generally hostile stance towards trade unions should not be seen as an automatic by-product of the spread of HRM, but rather as a predictable development in its own right, given the events of recent history, the political climate and the economic pressures upon companies. These were, then, two logically separate developments, although as we shall see they interacted in a number of subtle ways.

Storey's study bears out the thesis that a predominant mode in mainstream organisations was the *marginalisation* of trade unions and of industrial relations: they just came to figure much less prominently on the managerial list of priorities as they were crowded out by other concerns.

On the one hand this could be seen as a process of general neglect at a time when managers were simply too preoccupied with other matters. On the other hand it could on occasion appear to be part of a more deliberate policy of locking unions into discussion of increasingly trivial issues as a way of keeping them away from discussion of more strategic concerns. Storey cites canteens, locker room facilities, car parking and regulation of contract work as recurring examples of such issues and quotes a plant manager commenting cheerfully: 'Well I'd rather keep them busy on such matters than get us involved in anything too heavy!'[4]

This developing picture contains a fair amount of managerial opportunism and pragmatism, but Storey is at pains to point out that it is not enough simply to characterise managerial approaches to workplace relations as 'pragmatic', implying no overall sense of direction – as tended to be argued in the mid-1980s for example. Though the pragmatic flavour was still in evidence by the time of his study, 'the famed pragmatism has moved to a new centre of gravity'. He goes on to give four indicators of the direction and nature of that movement:[5]

- Labour relations 'firefighting' has been pushed to the extreme margins of management concern.
- A reasonably consistent set of aspirations and understandings grew and spread of what 'management' should be doing and, as part of this, what people-management should look like.

■ This new understanding was spread in particular by an increase in the volume and frequency of messages coming down from more senior levels.

■ Communications were reinforced by concrete measures such as site closures, demanning, delayering, more formal target setting, closer monitoring of performance and moves towards linking performance to rewards.

THE NEW MAINSTREAM

This all tends to confirm the emerging view about what now constitutes the mainstream territory within which, typically, organisations are going to choose the basis on which they conduct their relationships with their employees.

The spectrum of mainstream choice has, at one end, the 'non-union private sector' accounting for a large swathe of the economy and containing within it the profile of low-technology, insecure employment, summarised at the end of the previous chapter. Next to it comes the still relatively unusual – but more frequent than was previously realised – cases of outright derecognition of trade unions and the replacing of a previously pluralist set of arrangements with a wholly unitarist regime.

There follows the 'greenfield site' territory. In the recession of the early 1990s this segment has been largely empty. In the post-recession period, however, the prediction is that the trends of the last decade will reassert themselves and employers will choose between a firmly non-union approach – accompanied in some but by no means all sectors by relatively sophisticated and individualistic HR strategies – and the single union deal.

Now we come to the territory characterised by fairly traditional formal structures of industrial relations but in which the attitude of the employer is of sustained and visible hostility to the trade unions. This is where 'hard HRM' merges into old-style aggressive industrial relations management. The data from the 1990 Workplace Industrial Relations Survey suggests, interestingly in this respect, that the adoption of features of HRM was most common in workplaces with recognised trade unions.

Alongside this is a segment of firms in which industrial relations structures and processes survive but are the subject of massive managerial indifference. The industrial relations director of the UK subsidiary of a large multinational company put the point this way:[6]

I have to spend a proportion of my time dealing with the trade unions – I don't like it but it's my job. I'm very aware that most of my management colleagues think that unions and all that they are associated with are completely alien and incomprehensible. They just can't understand why we should spend any time dealing with them at all. We tolerate unions because basically they are there, and we continue to tolerate them for as long as they don't cause us any trouble. If they ever did cause trouble – obstructed our plans, went on strike, yes, actually behaved like unions – I would be under tremendous pressure to get rid of them straight away.

And finally we can find at the extreme end of the spectrum a relatively small number of organisations who seek actively to involve their employees' trade unions in their plans for change. The worrying feature for unions, however, is the smallness of this category and the apparent fact that the overwhelming majority of employers with whom they deal, and on whom they rely organisationally and financially, view them with, at best, indifference and, at worst, outright antipathy.

For these same employers the point can be put the other way around: they are locked into relationships and structures that dominate their dealings with their employees but out of which they feel that they get little value and which they find difficult, if not impossible, to put to active use as a vehicle through which they can achieve constructive change.

So how did we get here? How did employers choose where to place themselves on this spectrum? And more to the point, what will determine their choice in the future?

Looking back over the last decade and a half we find that, in broad terms, many employers have taken a tactical judgement on whether they can introduce the changes which they feel that they need, and gain the requisite degree of commitment from the workforce, without having to engineer major changes in employee relations structures and procedures – by, for example, having to derecognise trade unions. If they cannot, then very often they have set about replacing their pluralistic structures with ones that are essentially unitarist – controlled and directed by the employer and designed for the express purpose of implementing the employer's policy, rather than representing and reaching accommodations between diverging interests.

If on the other hand they judge that they can get away without any great structural change, then the typical result will be what has been termed 'dualism' – in which change programmes, with a real bearing on the substance of the relationship between employer and employed, are driven through by managers and joint working parties, often under the banner of HRM, with a rump system of industrial relations left discussing the annual pay award and some not very glamorous aspects of the physical working environment.

The third approach has been in those few instances where employers have actively encouraged trade unions to become involved in the change process – to become 'partners in change' in the manner advocated in the 'management by agreement' literature of the 1970s. Rare though it might have been, some notable examples of the approach can still be found – not just in the public sector, where high levels of unionisation and industrial relations constitutionalism continue to prevail – but also in some major private sector companies, such as Ford and Rover. Both of these organisations consciously set out to involve their trade unions in the design and implementation of far-reaching programmes of employment change. In the case of Rover the programme was designed to introduce 'Japanese-style' working practices and production techniques. In the case of Ford the aim was to boost productivity and transform the approach to supervision.

Looking ahead it is hard to envisage any significant change in this picture which would either enlarge the area of the spectrum covered by pluralist relationships or which would dilute the mixture of indifference and hostility that seems to characterise the attitude of so many UK managers to the idea of dealing with trade unions (even when they continue formally to recognise them).

On the one hand it seems that it is mostly inertia that continues to sustain a high proportion of the established union/management structures – an unenthusiastic but businesslike judgement that the cost of change and disruption outweighs the benefit of starting with a fresh sheet of paper. On the other hand the more active forces at work are either straightforwardly hostile to the pluralist notions that have sustained traditional industrial relations (as is the case in the non-union private sector), or are concerned with the more individualistic aspects of HRM, to which trade unionism as it has been practised in the past has found it most difficult to relate with any real purpose.

In short, looking across the spectrum of mainstream employer choice the tide seems clearly to be running against the pluralist concepts and structures on which our industrial relations have been founded in the past. And as it runs out there is the prospect that the position of trade unionism will come to resemble, not so much a monolith as a scattered set of islands surrounded by a very unitarist, and mostly hostile, ocean. Nor is this a surprising conclusion to reach given the motivation of the principal groups of employers that we have considered.

For many employers in the *non-union private sector*, the driving force is cost reduction and flexible use of resources – especially labour. This position is compatible with a hard-nosed industrial relations approach, but increasingly some employers have focused on the additional *control* that they would gain over resource allocation and costs in the absence of unions.

Those organisations that are embracing, or have embraced, the more integrative and individualistic features of HRM are likely to find unions at best an inescapable part of the institutional furniture, to be bypassed wherever possible using new communications techniques, or otherwise an irrelevant and time-consuming sideshow to the main business on their agenda.

Then there are the organisations that are concentrating hard on the concept of 'empowering' their workforces as a strategy to achieve change. These organisations often talk about 'empowerment' in terms which sound, initially at least, as if they allow for a pluralistic basis for the relationship between employer and employed. After all, is not empowerment consistent with the idea of independence and of autonomy; and might not this seem logically therefore to extend to the notion of an 'empowered' workforce having its own representative structure and voice?

FOCUS ON EMPOWERMENT

One problem in getting to grips with this issue is the notoriously elusive quality of the 'empowerment' vocabulary: even by the standards of management jargon this is a slippery concept, apparently used by different people to convey many quite different meanings.

In an attempt to clarify matters Figure 6.1 shows what appears to be a spectrum of different ways in which the concept of empowerment is employed. The variable is the range or depth of the organisation's activities over which the workforce is empowered to exert their influence. Thus at one end of the scale 'empowerment' is about giving individuals a 'say' by empowering them to make suggestions over local issues. Further along the scale local workgroups are given the opportunity and authority to design or redesign their bit of the work system, but within a tight framework of performance targets and without the ability to influence wider aspects of the work system or the policies and strategies that underpin them. As we move rightwards along the spectrum empowerment connotes an ability to influence wider and deeper aspects of the organisation's activities.

At the right hand end of the scale we *appear* to be in territory that shares assumptions with the 'management by agreement' thinking of earlier periods. 'Empowerment' here can cover quite fundamental aspects of the organisation's goals, operations and policies, and it might be argued that the only effective way to organise this and make it happen is by creating a representative structure and voice for the empowered workforce – very much on pluralist lines. This is not typically, however, what employers have in mind when they talk about empowerment – even at the right hand end of the scale. Their purpose is *not* to share power with an alternative and parallel source of legitimacy and authority within

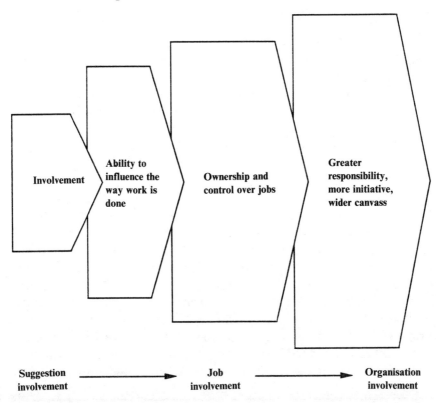

Involvement | Ability to influence the way work is done | Ownership and control over jobs | Greater responsibility, more initiative, wider canvass

Suggestion involvement ⟶ Job involvement ⟶ Organisation involvement

Figure 6.1 The empowerment spectrum

the organisation. Rather it is to give employees the opportunity, authority and space to direct their energies towards improving the performance of the organisation and to remove problems and obstacles which stand in the way of competitive success (including those that arise from trade union agreements).

Put in these terms, 'empowerment' comes across with distinctly unitarist overtones. From the employer's point of view the difficulty of trying to relate their interest in empowering employees to more traditional industrial relations concepts based on the notion of 'representation' is that there is a mismatch of level and of interest. Empowerment is either about very local, very specific, very practical problem-solving (the left hand end of the spectrum above) or, at the other end, it is about not just expressing a view about the organisation's direction and management but actually about taking some responsibility for them. Richard Block in his book, *The Empowered Manager*, says that the goal 'is to have all members believe and act like this is their organisation and to take personal responsibility for how it operates'.[7]

It is this sense of creating 'ownership' of problems and of the search for solutions that sits most uneasily with conventional pluralist notions of the workforce being *represented*, in Hugh Clegg's famous phrase, by 'an opposition that does not seek to govern'. The issues of *trust* and of *power* come to the surface at this point. The pluralist arrangement that Clegg[8] was characterising had a sense of a balance of power between two organised interests and a sufficient degree of trust within the relationship (usually) for each side to respect the other's legitimate and, on occasions, separate interests, and for both sides to refrain from pushing their interest separately to the point where it became impossible to keep the whole show on the road. The degree of trust was limited however and constrained either side from 'trespassing' on the domain of the other: hence the notion of the 'frontier of control', coined by G D H Cole, dividing an area of managerial prerogative from an area policed by joint agreements and custom and practice.

As we move across to the 'empowerment' model the degree of trust embodied in the system *appears* to be higher. Managers are prepared to 'let go' of more areas of control and decision-making to empowered workers. They in turn are led to trust that managers will respect the results of their work. The sense of a power balance is entirely lacking, however. The goal, as Block says, is to achieve a sense of ownership, but, except very occasionally, the employer is not interested in spreading ownership itself. Can this trick be pulled off? A key question – and one to which we shall return below – is whether in the absence of a pluralist system of 'checks and balances' sufficient trust can be generated to enable the 'empowerment' approach to deliver what employers want from it.

A CLEAR WAY FORWARD?

How should we react to this picture of the new mainstream of employer choice? What should we make of the fact that pluralism, as the basis for structuring employment relationships, appears to be in long-term decline? What conclusions should we draw from the growing size of the non-union private sector or from the 'dualism' that has grown up, even where unions continue to be recognised? How does the notion of 'empowerment' fit into all this?

One conclusion might be that this is all fine and represents a positive way forward. Pluralism and the industrial relations structures that went with it only flourished, goes this argument, because of a lack of management grip. Employers lacked either the willingness or the skill to engage in the *direct* management of their workforces and so, in effect, subcontracted it out to collective agreements. This was always second best and so the fact that an increasing number of employers are rolling their sleeves up and tackling the management of their employees directly, pushing aside the institutions and procedures that got in the way of this relationship, is a good thing.

Moreover, runs this argument, the fact that we see a wide variation in the employee relations arrangements that are springing up is a healthy sign. The name of the game is, after all, employer choice – that has been the central thrust of the legislation that has rewritten the employee relations rulebook in the last decade and a half. So if some employers choose to conduct their relationships with their workforce directly, on their own terms and without the intervention of 'external' forces such as trade unions, that is their business. In just the same way, if other employers decide that it suits their needs, on balance, to continue to work through a collective relationship with a trade union, that too is a business judgement that they will make on the basis of the circumstances facing them at that time. (The case studies in Chapter 7 illuminate this theme clearly).

There are counter-arguments to this view, however: arguments that raise questions about whether the emerging pattern of choice depicted here is quite so unambiguously 'a good thing'.

In the first place it can be argued that the duality depicted above, in which employers maintain the formal structures of pluralist industrial relations but for the most part marginalise it – consigning it to dealing with the local and trivial while the strategic issues are handled through unitarist, employer-controlled mechanisms – is a wasteful instance of muddle and missed opportunity. Even when marginalised, these structures continue to be the decisive influence over terms and conditions of employment. To disengage these areas therefore from the processes that 'really matter' – those through which the organisation is to grapple with fundamental business change issues – is somehow to send a very mixed message. For many employees the measure of whether something is truly important is whether it impacts directly on their contractual relationship with their employer. To be told, therefore, that a change programme is of over-arching importance but to learn that the programme does not engage with the processes and mechanisms by which your employment position is determined, and through which your voice is heard, may appear as a contradiction.

Certainly, runs the argument, such a state of affairs is symptomatic of an incompleteness in the organisation's approach to change – a failure to integrate and use all the mechanisms for change that are available to it and to follow change through from the strategic visions of the boardroom to the daily reality of the employment contracts of the workplace.

A second counter-argument applies in relation to organisations that adopt a straightforwardly unitarist approach: conducting their employee relations on the explicit premise that there is room for only one interest – the interest of the organisation as a business entity – and that that interest is articulated and steered from the top of the organisation, with employment policies being geared to achieving the best 'fit' of the workforce to the organisation's goals and to maximise their contribution to its competitive success. There are three components to this argument:

1. With sufficient investment and the application of professional human resource policies in the fields of communication, performance management and training, such an approach is *feasible and viable* – as shown by the large number of organisations that either moved in this direction during the 1980s or started from scratch on this basis. However...

2. There is a danger with this approach of over-promising: of

fostering a view that, having taken on the full mantle of responsibility for the management of employment issues the employer is somehow capable of over-riding economic forces and giving guarantees about security and about development which cannot, in practice, be fulfilled. This has led in some instances to a considerable degree of *cynicism* when the panoply of employment policies erected under the HRM banner, with its promise that 'people are our greatest asset', gave way to job loss and redundancy during the recession of the 1990s.

3. The *investment* in time, effort, communication, listening and, above all, in management skill required to run a de-centralised, unitarist employee relations regime effectively is easy to underestimate. Moreover, within the prevailing management culture of many British organisations, with its emphasis on short-term financial returns, its 'command and control' instinct towards work organisation and its discomfort with all the 'touchy-feely' connotations of the softer, developmental aspects of HRM, such investment is always going to be under pressure and likely to be squeezed. The consequent danger is that organisations will open up a huge gap between the rhetoric and the reality of their employment practices. Under pressure, and in the absence of the countervailing force that an independent employee 'voice' can provide, managers who have learned the language of 'culture change' of 'empowerment' and of 'investing in people', but have not undertaken the transformation in *their* role and behaviour required to make a reality of these concepts will revert to type. More precisely, they will revert to Type X: behaviour based on the assumption that employees are inherently untrustworthy and in need of discipline, control and sanctions in order to make them do as they should.

THE IMPORTANCE OF 'VOICE'

This adds up to a recipe for a more oppressive and unpleasant workplace. There is also, however, a strong and developed argument to say that it also leads to a more *inefficient* workplace. This proposition at first runs counter to the widely-held view that managerial assertiveness – 'strong' management – is associated with high productivity whereas the presence of trade unions is an indicator of inefficiency, restrictive practices and low productivity.

The qualifications to this view have been expressed by the writers of the Harvard School in the US – most notably by Freeman and Medoff.[9] Their starting point is that trade unions, particularly in large enterprises, provide workers as a group with a means of communicating with management – a collective 'voice' – which can help bring actual and desired conditions closer together on a less costly basis than the classic free market mechanism of exit-and-entry: by analogy, 'discussing marital problems rather than going directly to the divorce court', or, more directly, 'discussing with an employer conditions that ought to be changed, rather than quitting the job'.

At the workplace, argue Freeman and Medoff, collective rather than individual bargaining with an employer is a necessary condition for the establishment of an effective 'voice' mechanism for two reasons:

■ Workers who are tied to a firm will be reluctant to express their true feelings and preferences for fear that the employer may fire them or otherwise disadvantage them.

■ Many important features of the workplace fall into the category of 'public goods', that is items such as safety provision, lighting, heating, training: all things which affect everyone in the group, (and which add to the productivity of the workplace), but on which, without a collective voice, the incentive for the individual to express his or her preferences or to invest time and money in changing conditions is likely to be too small to spur action.

Freeman and Medoff[10] go on to draw out the following implications from this analysis.

In a non-union setting, where exit-and-entry is the predominant form of adjustment, the signals and incentives to firms depend on the preferences of the 'marginal' worker, the one who might leave because of (or be attracted by) small changes in the conditions of employment. The firm responds to the needs of this marginal worker, who is generally young and marketable; the firm can to a considerable extent ignore the preferences of typically older, less marketable workers, who – for reasons of skill, knowledge, rights that cannot readily be transferred to other enterprises, as well as because of other costs associated with changing firms – are effectively immobile. In a unionised setting, by contrast, the union takes account of *all* workers in determining its demands at the bargaining table, so that the desires of workers who are highly unlikely to leave the enterprise are also represented...

Under some conditions, the union contract – by taking account of all workers and by appropriately considering the sum of preferences for work conditions that are common to all workers – *can be economically more efficient* than the contract that would result in the absence of unions.

The sources of the extra efficiency that this collective union voice can provide include the following:

- The extra *information* about the operation of the workplace and of the production process that can be made available to managements through the dialogue that is engendered.
- The reduction in the rate of *quitting* that is empirically associated with trade unionism and the consequent reduction in hiring and training costs and the disruption associated with higher turnover.
- The greater productivity that seems to be associated with both the introduction of formal *grievance and arbitration procedures* and the move towards personnel policies that are based more on *seniority* and less on discretion – both moves bearing connotations of greater fairness and even-handedness.

As against this, of course, it must be recognised that there are many organisations for whom the 'marginal' worker described above is seen as absolutely key to the firm's success and who would view seniority-based policies with horror: as a certain recipe for bureaucracy, 'buggins turn' and the triumph of mediocrity over high performance. Nonetheless Freeman and Medoff[11] make a well argued and empirically supported case that under the right circumstances the collective 'voice' of trade unions can add measurably to an organisation's performance. They also deal with the follow-on question: if a collective voice is necessary, is it necessary for it to be provided by a trade union?

> For such systems to work, management must give up power and accept a dual authority channel within the firm. Such a change in power is difficult to attain in the absence of a genuine independent union or union-like organisation... The problem is akin to that of operating a democratic parliament in a monarchical or dictatorial regime. As long as the monarch or the dictator has the final word, the parliament cannot truly function. (p 108)

This is to put the point in quite stark terms – as if the employer can never, through his or her own actions, substitute for the advantages that an independent trade union voice can bring to the workforce and to the workplace. Another way of approaching the point is to see the argument as a *challenge* for an employer. What does the employer need to do in order to leave employees believing that there is nothing more that a union could contribute?

PUBLIC GOODS AND PRIVATE INTERESTS

So, there is an argument to be made that in the right conditions, and managed properly, the existence of a pluralist 'collective voice' for the workforce, in the shape of an independent trade union, *can* improve the efficiency of the workplace. It can moreover contribute to the solution of economy-wide problems – in the UK the weakness of vocational training and consequent skill shortages are the obvious examples – that are made worse rather than better by the internalisation of industrial relations structures and the removal of multi-employer mechanisms.

The trouble with this argument is that for many businessmen it will never pass the 'so what?' test. It is an argument that seems to belong in the abstract and theoretical world of the 'public good' and to have little bearing on the urgent, immediate issues facing their businesses. As we have seen in this chapter, they see their priorities as establishing direct, closely-managed relationships with 'their' employees (cutting out the 'boundaries') in order to increase the flexibility of work and the responsiveness of work processes to customer needs.

Moreover, as we have seen in earlier chapters the general disposition of managers in the post-war decades to see trade unions as natural parts of the business landscape – to be worked with in the pursuit of solutions to problems – has given way to an attitude that is at best indifferent and often downright hostile to trade unions: seeing them as impediments to the pursuit of business goals. Against this background the argument for a more pluralist approach will often be drowned out or simply ignored.

In the UK business context one of the weaknesses of the pluralist case is the relative absence of 'success stories' – widely recognised instances of organisations setting out to work in partnership with trade unions and, by doing so, successfully raising the organisation's performance and giving it an improved competitive edge. In this chapter, the work redesign projects at Ford and Rover have been mentioned as examples of this approach, and there are other instances to be found both in the public sector and in other parts of manufacturing. Such examples are, however, thin on the ground in the UK. One of the clearest recent cases to be described may seem rather distant to many British managers, because it comes from the US, but it merits reflection because it pulls so many of the threads of this chapter together in one specific example.

The case concerns a car plant in Fremont, California – the site of a joint venture between General Motors and Toyota called New United Motor Manufacturing Inc (NUMMI). The plant has been shaped around the full panoply of Japanese production techniques. The workforce is organised into teams – teams, moreover, who are empowered to design their own part of the production process and to set production standards themselves. The job of management is to support the production teams with problem-solving expertise. Under this new regime the Fremont plant has been transformed from its previous status within GM folklore as 'the worst plant in the world', with abysmally low levels of productivity, quality and attendance and abysmally high levels of drug and alcohol abuse, union militancy and strikes. It enjoys productivity and quality levels which are higher than any other GM plant and almost as high as Toyota's Japanese plants.

And here's the rub. This was achieved by employing virtually all of the previous workforce including the old union representatives. The United Auto Workers Union was made sole bargaining agent, was deeply involved in the selection and training of staff (and managers) and was able to influence just about every aspect of the process by which the plant was transformed from 'dog' to 'star'.

Writing about this case in the *Harvard Business Review*, Professor Paul Adler[12] noted the paradox that whereas many observers assume that the discipline of Toyota-style operations requires tight control by management over the workforce and the elimination of independent workforce and trade union power, at NUMMI the power of the union and its members has actually increased. In fact, concludes Professor Adler, 'it may be that the NUMMI model has succeeded only *because* of this high level of worker and union power'. Here is his argument:

> What makes the NUMMI production system so enormously effective is its ability to make production problems immediately visible and to mobilise the power of teamwork. Implemented with trust and respect, both these features of the system create real empowerment. Wielded autocratically, they would have the opposite effect... Teamwork could become a means of mobilising peer pressure. A healthy level of challenge could degenerate into stress and anxiety.

The NUMMI production system thus gives managers enormous potential control over workers. With this potential power ready at hand, and under pressure to improve business performance, there is a real danger that the relationship will sooner or later slide back into the old coercive pattern.

But such a slide would have an immediate and substantial negative impact on business performance, because labour would respond in kind. An alienated workforce wipes out the very foundation of continuous improvement and dries up the flow of worker suggestions that fuel it. And the lack of inventory buffers means that disaffected workers could easily bring the whole just-in-time production system to a grinding halt.

In other words, NUMMI's production system increases the power both of management over workers and of workers over management. *A system this highly charged needs a robust governance process in which the voices of management and labour can be clearly heard and effectively harmonised on high-level policy issues as well as on work-team operating issues. The union gives workers this voice ... In this way, the union not only serves workers' special interests, it also serves the larger strategic goals of the business by effectively depriving management of absolute domain and helping to maintain management discipline.*

These points are important to bear in mind as we look, first, at some cases of employee relations change in UK companies and then at the implications of this chapter – concerned as it has been with the range of choices now open to employers – for the future of trade unions.

References

1. IPM/NEDO (1992) *Performance Management in the UK*, IPM, London
2. Millward, N, Stevens, M, Smart, D and Hawes, W R (1992) *Workplace Industrial Relations In Transition, The ED/ESRC/PSI/ ACAS Surveys*, Dartmouth Publishing Company Ltd, Aldershot
3. Storey, J (1992) *Developments in the Management of Human Resources*, Blackwell, Oxford, pp 246–7
4. Ibid. p 257
5. Ibid. p 260
6. Private interview with author
7. Block, R (1991) *The Empowered Manager*, Paramount Books, Hemel Hempstead
8. Clegg, H (1976) *The System of Industrial Relations in Great Britain*, Blackwell, Oxford

9. Freeman, R and Medoff, J (1984) *What do Unions do?*, Basic Books, New York
10. Ibid. p 10, emphasis added
11. Ibid. p 108
12. Adler, P (1993) *Harvard Business Review*, Jan/Feb 1993, p 107, emphasis added

CHAPTER 7

Case Studies

INTRODUCTION

In this chapter we take a close-up look at a number of organisations that have undergone major change in the recent past and
which, as part of that change, have refashioned important aspects
of their employee relations.

The idea here is *not* to present the case studies as if they are part
of a representative sample survey. The cases have been chosen
because, in their different ways, each provides a clear practical
instance of an organisation implementing one or other of the
approaches discussed in more theoretical terms in the previous
chapters.

Thus, in the case of *Organisation A* we see a company pushing
through a policy of deunionisation as part of a major programme
of changes to work organisation and production methods. In the
case of H&R Johnson, by contrast we see a firm facing a similar
range of business issues and a corresponding need to change the
way in which it managed its relationship with its workforce. In this
case, however, the decision was taken to work with the trade
unions rather than derecognising them: albeit that key features of
the relationship were redefined and the company successfully
'internalised' its industrial relations – pulling out of the national
industry collective agreement.

The third case, Air Products, makes something of a distinction
between its approach to its management and staff grades, where
sophisticated HRM techniques are applied on a highly individualised basis, and its manual workforce – with whom it retains a
collectively organised and regulated relationship. The distinctive
feature here, however, is the redefinition of the content and climate
of the employment relationship within this traditional industrial
relations structure.

In each case we are looking at the practical dynamics of change – how did it actually happen in practice, and what lessons can practitioners learn from other organisations.

ORGANISATION A

Background

This company is, among other things, a major manufacturer of parts for the motor industry. Its links with the motor industry were personified by the experience and outlook of many members of its management team and were shown in the employment conditions and pay of its workforce as well as in its industrial relations arrangements.

The challenge, as defined by the company, was to change this state of affairs: to change business and working practices, and, more fundamentally, to change the attitudes and culture which underpinned them and which were now seen as inappropriate to the business conditions facing the company. A programme of change was initiated which brought about a series of radical shifts in working practices and processes and which also brought about, on the way, the withdrawal of all trade union recognition: a measure which would have been hard to imagine a few years earlier.

The business drivers

Unionisation of the company's staff followed a pattern which largely reflected the motor industry background. High levels of union membership were found among the hourly-paid staff (mostly TGWU, but with AEU and other craft union representation as well) while something over one third of non-manual employees were unionised (mostly APEX, but some MSF and some ACTSS).

From the management's perspective, unionisation raised rather separate issues in different parts of the group. An ageing Midlands manufacturing site was seen as having a rather dormant, inactive style of trade unionism and an ossified set of inappropriate consultation arrangements, which offered little back by way of workforce engagement or enthusiasm. The key question was therefore whether there was a justifiable payback to the company for their investment in maintaining a highly regulated industrial relations regime.

Elsewhere the perception was that trade unionism was active but not in ways that benefited the company. The regulation of working practices was strongly entrenched and vigorously defended. It covered areas such as the allocation of work duties, overtime, and selection for promotion, which a new management team, largely drawn from sectors such as retail and distribution, were inclined to see as lying within the sphere of management discretion. This perception was heightened by the amount of time taken up in meetings with the shop stewards, who had extensive facilities on all sites.

Such a state of affairs might have remained broadly unquestioned in a period of business stability, but for the company this was a period of considerable turbulence. The forces driving them in the direction of change included:

- *Industry restructuring.* The growth of the Japanese car manufacturers, and the growing influence of the component manufacturers associated with them, as well as changes in the respective fortunes of the more traditional UK-based manufacturers all contributed to a more competitive market place, with pressure on costs and other aspects of performance. Reduction in inventory levels and in work in process, and adherence to increasingly challenging just-in-time delivery schedules had become absolutely crucial to the business's position.
- *Quality.* The increasing emphasis on quality throughout the industry, together with the partnership or 'stakeholder' philosophy governing relations between suppliers and manufacturers, had put the spotlight on working practices and in particular on the need for greater flexibility and responsiveness.
- *Service standards.* A key aspect of competitive performance had been the need to reduce delivery times to customers. This put a premium on flexibility in working practices, working hours and shift systems.
- *Technology.* In warehousing and manufacturing alike there were major-step changes in industry-standard technology which forced a complete rethink in the way in which work was organised and in staffing and skill levels. Flexibility and multi-skilled team working came to be seen as the prerequisites for success.

Planning the change

Taken together, these trends and developments presented the company with the requirement for a major-step change in the way in which work was organised and carried out. This change had two aspects: on the one hand a far greater emphasis on flexibility, responsiveness and timeliness in the technical organisation of work, on the other hand a transformation in attitude and culture with the stress firmly on accountability, problem solving and commitment to the firm's success.

Faced with this changing performance requirement the company set up a project team, which progressively involved the key line managers, to identify the competitive practices and attitudes that needed to be put in place to achieve world-class performance. This in turn produced an analysis of the extent of the changes in working practices that this would require and the employee relations implications. The following employment policies were identified as being central to the company's new direction:

■ Individual performance appraisal.
■ Performance related pay.
■ Team working and the introduction of 'team leaders'.
■ Team briefing.
■ A big investment in training and development.
■ A massive increase in communications to staff.

Having identified these key elements the company considered the likely reaction of their local union shop stewards; would they be positive, negative or indifferent. Their conclusion was that the changes that they wanted most were the ones that would be resisted most actively by the unions. They also concluded that the procedures, practices and culture bound up with union recognition would add nothing to the company's drive to raise its performance in a significant way. In their view, at a time when the company was embarking on a major change in the way in which people delivered their work and in the way in which production was controlled – with a move away from traditional systems of supervision and inspection and towards a more 'empowered', self-directed approach – trade unions would add nothing positive to the process. Worse, the antagonism that they might display towards key aspects of the changes could lead to waste of precious management time in lengthy negotiations.

Making the change

The change programme was introduced more or less simultaneously across the company. The future of the Midlands manufacturing plant had been in doubt for some time, and the uncertainty felt by the workforce had grown accordingly.

Rather to the surprise, and certainly much to the relief, of the workforce the managing director then announced that the future of the factory was to be secured with a multi-million pound investment programme. A package of measures was to accompany this investment, the principal components of which were:

- A large-scale extension of the 'Japanese style' production methods and working practices, including Kanban working, just-in-time production and team working, with supervisory levels stripped out.
- The introduction of quality groups, reinforced by the reward and recognition system.
- A pledge that if the need for workforce reductions arose they would be handled by seeking redeployment and reskilling.
- The replacement of payment by results by a consolidated basic wage and performance related pay.
- The introduction of performance appraisal for all employees.
- A major communications programme, centred around team briefings. This involved daily team briefings, monthly team meetings, staff conferences and the frequent use of questionnaires and attitude surveys.
- A major investment in training and development.
- An end to trade union recognition. Staff forums were to be introduced as a vehicle for consultation, with representation on a constituency basis.

Embedded as it was in a package of changes that offered the workforce new hope for their future, the derecognition of unions created little adverse reaction. Employees were offered new contracts incorporating the changes, and all had signed them within three months.

In the warehousing and distribution areas, the ending of union recognition came about in a similar manner. The workforce were issued with new contracts which, among an extensive set of employment changes, excluded trade union recognition. Again they were given six months notice and, again, the vast majority of the workforce signed up.

Having dislodged the trade unions from the main centres of manual employment it was then almost a matter of routine to end their recognition in respect of non-manual staff, only around one third of whom actually belonged to a trade union.

As with the manufacturing plant, union derecognition came as part of a more wide-ranging package of employment policy changes. Moreover, in this case elements of the package were centred around the perceived desirability of creating more family involvement in the life of the company – of integrating work with other spheres of life. An example was the creation of a scheme of educational support for 16–19 year old family members; another was the introduction of family open days.

Life without unions

As far as the company's management is concerned, the period since derecognition has been marked by successful progress towards their business objectives.

- Performance appraisal and performance related pay have been implemented for all employees.
- The company's particular approach to quality circles has taken root and has produced a flow of valuable proposals. As a result work processes have been improved significantly and savings worth £3 million have been identified.
- An extensive communications process, owned and controlled by line management, and involving team briefings, monthly team meetings, questionnaire research, and an information forum, has replaced the formalised union-based structure of the past.
- Team-based working structures, together with team leaders, have been introduced.
- Training and individual development have been extended significantly.

In this same period the business has seen a 40 per cent improvement in productivity. The company believes that the morale of the workforce is good and that changes made to the physical environment and amenities of the site have been popular. The changes introduced have put a strong spotlight on the management style and capacity of the organisation. Indeed a radical shift in management style has been required, with managers needing to be more visible, more accountable and more approachable in order to handle the new relationship with their staff.

Could these benefits have been won without the derecognition of the trade unions? How central was this aspect of the programme to the realisation of the gains? The full-time officials of the unions

concerned were adamant that all of the changes in working practices that the company were seeking could have been achieved
through negotiation. Indeed, they were at pains to point out that at
the very time when the company was pushing through their
changes, the same officials of the same unions were negotiating the
introduction of a more or less identical package of measures less
than a mile away at a vehicle manufacturing factory. In their view
the company's insistence on derecognition was not primarily
business-driven; rather it reflected an innate hostility to unions on
the part of some of the company's senior managers – particularly
those who came from outside the industry.

The company would put the point differently. They would
acknowledge the close parallels between their package of changes
and those which were introduced through negotiation elsewhere.
They would, however, point to the amount of time and effort that
they would have had to expend in negotiations if they had gone
down that route and would question whether, in the end, this
process really would have produced a significantly greater level of
commitment on the part of the workforce to the changes themselves. As far as they were concerned the situation was clear. The
frustration and time involved in working through the trade unions
was simply not matched by any corresponding business benefit: the
game, bluntly, was not worth the candle.

Moreover the company calculated correctly that they could end
their relationship with the trade unions without incurring any great
cost to themselves. In the event it was all surprisingly easy.

Derecognition was, for the company, something which became
the logical consequence of a set of far-reaching changes in production methods and working practices to which they were driven
by powerful competitive pressures. It was also a symbolic step, one
that demonstrated management determination to follow through
on the required changes. At a certain stage in the process of change
the company arrived at a judgement that their interests would best
be served by discontinuing their relationship with the trade unions.
Having taken that step they simply proceeded with the implementation of the rest of their programme.

H&R JOHNSON

Background

H&R Johnson is a long-established and major component of the ceramics industry. Based in the Potteries area of Staffordshire since 1901, and, since 1979, a member of the Norcros group of companies, H&R Johnson is the largest UK manufacturer of ceramic wall and floor tiles. It has a dominant share of the UK market as well as a growing export trade, which now makes up some 20 per cent of the company's sales.

Since the late 1980s the company has been through a series of far-reaching changes in its production and working practices which, among other things, has manifested itself in 'The Johnson Accord' – a complete recasting of the terms, conditions and procedures governing relations with the workforce. The Accord seeks to introduce not only a much simplified payment system and grade structure, but also (as with Organisation A) performance appraisal for manual workers. Unlike Organisation A, however, H&R Johnson consciously chose not to follow the path of union derecognition in pursuing their restructuring. Instead they focused in on the advantages of pulling out from the industry-wide collective agreement and establishing their own tailor-made alternative. Their strategy, in other words, was one of 'internalisation'.

There are two noteworthy background aspects to the company's employee relations strategy, which chime interestingly with Organisation A's experience. One concerns geography, the other concerns the sector background and outlook of some of the leading participants in the change process.

As far as geography is concerned, the Potteries is unique in the UK in the strength of the identity between the area and a particular industry. The degree of concentration of the ceramics and china industries on the six towns of Stoke-on-Trent is without parallel, and the dependence of the area on the trade is correspondingly high. This meant that the development of the region and the development of the industry were historically intermingled. Thus, for example, the Trade Association and the collective agreement which it sponsored were seen as bedrocks of the local economy.

In similar vein the industry's dominant trade union, the Ceramic and Allied Trades Union (CATU), is highly unusual in having a very strong degree of representation among the relatively immobile labour force of the area while being all but invisible beyond the geographical confines of the six towns. Its combination of a geo-graphically compact and readily serviceable membership base combined with the relatively-low cost of maintaining a small number of collective agreements have helped to make it one of the most financially viable trade unions in the UK.

The other notable background feature is that some of the senior managers most closely involved with the company's programme of change were brought in from the motor industry. In fact they had been involved in the planning within Rover which led to the decision to introduce a wide-ranging set of Japanese-style working practices, and to do it through negotiation with the trade unions: the very negotiations which were taking place while Organisation A was pushing ahead with derecognition.

The drivers for change

In the past the ceramics industry has been characterised by rela-tively labour-intensive production methods involving heavy physical labour rather than high workforce skill levels and by a considerable degree of supervisory oversight. During the twentieth century the industry has benefited from a series of separate, sometimes fashion-related, developments which gave it long periods of relatively untroubled growth and market buoyancy. These included the near-universal popularity of ceramic fireplace tiles in the 1920s and 1930s, the postwar building boom, and the 1970s explosion in DIY and home improvement.

By the late 1980s, however, the whole industry was confronted by very strong pressures for change. Foremost among them were the following:

■ Increased competition. The decline in UK construction industry activity together with competition in international markets put strong pressure on costs as well as on product quality.
■ Changes in technology. These had already led to an increasingly automated production process for tile manufacture – removing large amounts of manual labour from key areas such as stacking and handling. Looking ahead the company could foresee fur-ther waves of technological change as, for example, the long-standing 'twice fired' process for making tiles came increasingly to be replaced by a 'once fired' process in which all decoration and glaze is applied to a clay tile prior to being fired, and the 'biscuit' firing stage is cut out.

■ Shortening product life cycles. These reflect a greater degree of fashion-consciousness in the market place. They have put a premium on reducing the time taken to get a new product to market and, consequently, on making production methods more flexible.

Planning the change

H&R Johnson had been responding to these pressures for some time. They had cut costs and improved productivity considerably. A major investment programme in the 1980s had led to a considerable step up in production automation. Since the late 1980s the workforce had been cut from some 2300 to 1500 in three years.

The company's perception, however, was that more was needed, particularly in the field of working methods and practices. Although staff numbers and therefore labour costs had been reduced, the way in which work was organised and jobs were designed and carried out remained substantially unchanged. The payment system and structure was extremely complex and fragmented – indeed to the point where the company had an incomplete understanding of the make up of their labour costs.

The industry agreement, to which the company was party, imposed a daunting and rather antiquated set of procedural regulations on working practices and on terms and conditions of employment. It also produced a very time-consuming structure of industrial relations which involved the company first in industry-level negotiations and then in local negotiations to agree the interpretation of the terms of the industry deal for the company's specific circumstances. From the company's point of view this was both costly and antithetical to the need for rapid changes in production methods and manning.

The company agreed that a logical starting point for tackling this situation would be a review of the payment system. This would have an immediate payback in terms of greater paybill control, but it would, in addition, enable the company to get a closer grip on the pattern of working practices which underpinned and exacerbated the fragmented payment system.

As the review got under way a wider, more searching analysis of the company's relationship with its workforce began, prompted to some extent by the arrival of new senior members of the management team with a shared background in the motor industry.

Making the change

One of the issues which the company addressed early on in this process concerned its relationship with the trade unions. In a way which echoed the process undertaken by Organisation A's management team, H&R Johnson asked themselves what they gained from recognising trade unions and what, conversely, they would stand to lose if they were to withdraw that recognition. The balance sheet for them was a positive one. Union membership was high – CATU represented some 90 per cent of the manual workforce, and the MSF staff union had a presence among non-manual employees.

It was not just about numbers, however: the unions were seen as an integral and legitimate part of the fabric of the organisation with deep roots in the locality and the rest of the industry. An attack on the position of the unions, it was felt, would therefore be seen by employees as a hostile move against them and this might well engender a negative reaction against the company's plans for change. At the same time the company calculated that there were gains in prospect if they could take the unions with them. In particular the company stood to gain enhanced legitimacy and credibility for its plans in the eyes of the workforce if it could be seen to have gained some sort of endorsement, however passive, from the trade unions.

As it happened this conclusion was broadly in line with the thinking that had gone on within Rover (and to which the newly-arrived members of the management team had been party) leading up to the decision to seek a negotiated route to the introduction of Japanese-style working methods.

With this in mind the company embarked on a series of changes which fell under three broad headings: *structure, style* and *content*.

As far as *structure* was concerned the principal changes comprised the following:

■ Withdrawal from the industry agreement (though not from the employers' association) and the creation instead of a company-specific deal.
■ Movement towards 'single table' bargaining covering the whole company in the place of fragmented separate negotiations involving eight other negotiating groups.
■ A concentration on dealing with in-company union representatives rather than, as before, with 'outside' full time officials.

Changes in *style* were geared very much at breaking away from the long-standing and entrenched 'game of bluff' that had grown up around the negotiating relationship between the company's management and the workforce's representatives. From the company's point of view, past practice had encouraged the latter to work on the assumption that, whatever management might say, there would always be 'a little bit more' available at the eleventh hour. Apart from anything else this psychology tended to undermine the seriousness with which the company's pronouncements about future plans and strategies were taken by the workforce.

Johnson's management therefore set out to demonstrate through a series of episodes that, while they were keen to build positive working relationships with union representatives, the area over which they would actually concede joint regulation through negotiation would be limited, as would the number of iterations that they would go through during any negotiations. In the words of one of the members of the management team:

> We set out to show that we would say what we mean and mean what we say. It was a more forceful style, carrying the clear message that whilst we wanted to carry the unions along with us, if it came to it we would do it anyway. It made our discussions more meaningful and created much greater clarity.

In the company's eyes this approach has not resulted in a marginalisation of trade unionism in H&R Johnson. Meetings and discussions might be less frequent and certainly less time-consuming, but they are seen as more businesslike and engaged with the core issues facing the company. They are, in other words, very much part of the change process.

Communication is seen as a central component of the new style of employee relations in the company. The volume of communication has increased dramatically since the management set out upon the new path. A multi-channel approach towards communication has been used with a heavy emphasis on face-to-face contact between staff and their local managers. This put the spotlight on the communication skills of first line managers. The company has also made efforts to respond to the agenda of issues identified by staff as meriting greater communication (training opportunities is one example).

Changes in the substantive *content* of the employment relationship at H&R Johnson have been pursued vigorously, with the initial review of the payment system acting as a spur for a wide-ranging reform of terms and conditions of employment. These changes have been brought together in a framework, called The Johnson Accord: an enabling agreement between the company and the trade unions. The radical nature of the changes carried through by the company can be illustrated by some of the key components of the accord:

■ The consolidation of a wide range of supplementary and bonus payments into a much simplified pay structure.
■ A major reduction in the number of different job categories and grades, with the target of moving over an 18-month period to a structure comprising only two broad employee classifications (Manufacturing Employee and Commercial and Management Employee) and only two categories within each classification.
■ The acceptance of full mobility and flexibility between these classifications and categories, subject only to skills capability.
■ The establishment of regular team briefings for all staff.
■ The introduction of regular performance appraisals and development reviews for *all* employees.

The Accord is seen as a framework document, within which detailed discussion and negotiation will continue to take place in order to develop particular areas. It is therefore both a record of the detailed conclusions of the annual wage negotiations and a vehicle for continuing change in working practices within the company. In June 1991, a copy of the accord was sent to each member of the workforce, with a recommendation for acceptance from the union representatives, which was subsequently endorsed by ballot.

Looking to the future

As far as H&R Johnson is concerned the company has succeeded both in introducing an important set of specific changes to working practices and payment systems, designed to support key business goals, and in creating a new framework of employee relations which has the following characteristics:

■ It is *company-specific* and free from the influence of external, industry-wide arrangements.
■ It is *efficient* in terms of management time.
■ It provides the company with *credibility* in the eyes of the workforce through the involvement of union representatives in the design of changes.

■ It provides a greatly enhanced degree of *communications* in a manner that enables the company to control the agenda of what is actually communicated.

■ Above all, it provides the company with far greater *flexibility* than hitherto and the ability therefore to respond rapidly to changes in demand or in production technology.

Looking ahead therefore the company is working on the assumption that this framework – including the role that it contains for trade unions – will provide the support that it will need in tackling some of the major changes and challenges that it can foresee arising in the years ahead. First there will be the need for 'smarter' production processes, with a corresponding increase in the skill levels and training requirements of the workforce. Second the rate of diffusion of new technology will be high, with a consequent need to adjust working practices on a regular basis. And, third, there will be an increasing trend to devolve responsibility to 'empowered' workers and the need therefore to redesign roles and provide more development opportunities.

AIR PRODUCTS

Background

Our third case study company operates at the heart of the manufacturing sector. Its business, as described by a senior company executive, is 'to take God's air, clean it up, cool it down, separate it out, and then sell the component gases to industry'. The products that it supplies are of such strategic importance that the company calculates that if it were ever to stop production, large sections of industry would be at a complete standstill within ten days.

Air Products is an American-owned company that entered the UK market in the late 1950s in a deliberate attempt to take on the 'sleeping giant' that had traditionally monopolised the market – BOC. Having itself been responsible for bringing an element of competition into the industry, Air Products has, since the late 1970s, faced a continuous sharpening of competitive forces, accompanied by downward pressure on price and an ever-stronger emphasis on quality and customer service.

By the early 1990s the company enjoyed a share of some 22 per cent of the market in gas cylinders, and some 40 per cent of the bulk industrial gas market. Along the way it had shed some staff but employed still some 2000 employees in the UK, and a total of 5000 across Europe.

Industrial relations and human resource management

To an extent, Air Products displays some of the features of those companies that we have seen in earlier chapters who talk the language of HRM for their managerial cadres, but the language of industrial relations for the rest of their workforce. Only to an extent, however, and there are some interesting subtleties in the evolution of both the company's HR techniques and of its approach towards industrial relations.

The human resource policy priorities for managers are set in part by the company's need to develop a management cadre that can be mobile and effective on an international basis – helping to manage the operations of the various European subsidiaries and joint ventures. To that end Air Products has developed a sophisticated approach towards management succession planning and a performance management and reward system that reflects the performance of the company at various levels.

There is a European element also in the conduct of Air Products' industrial relations due, for example, to the need to take into account the requirements of legislation concerning works councils in some of the countries in which the company operates. Essentially, however, industrial relations policy is driven by local requirements (and without any prescription from the US parent).

In addition to a white collar group, Air Products recognises unions in two bargaining units; both have distinctive features, and both have been through interesting changes in recent years.

Craft workers

The first bargaining group covers some 2–300 highly-skilled engineering craft workers – welders, boilermakers and so on – who are highly mobile, travelling from site to site to install, maintain and repair plant and equipment. There are many traditional features of the company's relationship with this workgroup (whom it inherited in a takeover). The bargaining structure, for example, is fairly typical of the engineering industry. So too is the fact that the company bargains with the unions (GMB and AEEU) on an annual basis. This is a deliberate policy choice, marking a company preference for the regular contacts and dialogue of annual wage bargaining over longer term contracts. 'The negotiating process sharpens people up', commented a senior executive. 'The hearing improves on both sides.'

Other aspects are more novel, however, and reflect the principal force shaping the company's relationship with this group: the overwhelming need for employment flexibility and for very high quality of output. This pressure led Air Products some 20 years ago to sign, what was at the time, a pretty revolutionary agreement with the craft unions. In essence this agreement was a prototype for more recent 'flexibility' deals. In exchange for a payment of 20 per cent or so above the industry minimum time rate, the company gained a high degree of labour flexibility and mobility and a minimum amount of inter-trade demarcation.

As far as quality is concerned the company has been talking about quality management with this workgroup for eight years or so and has a structure of quality groups with whom it has a policy of 'opening the books'. Thus, within an industrial relations structure which looks from the outside to be very traditional, the company has introduced major innovations in the *content* of its relationship with a key group of employees in order to achieve its business objectives. Along the way it has built a record of harmonious industrial relations and good communications in a sector and geographical area (the workforce is based near Wrexham) not always renowned for such harmony.

The kings of the road

The other bargaining unit covers the Air Products delivery drivers – together with associated staff who work in loading bays and so on. Within the driving force there are cylinder truck drivers and then there are the real road kings – the drivers of the cryogenic tankers whose strategic importance is reflected in earnings of up to £28,000 pa.

The driving workforce is represented by the GMB, which enjoyed a full post-entry closed shop agreement when such things were legal. Now it just has 100 per cent membership! Here again the outward appearances are of a very traditional industrial relations set up. Negotiations are annual – and can be quite sharp. The payment system reflects a relationship between company and workforce which is heavily preoccupied with volume: there is a long-standing and satisfactory bonus scheme, which is geared to the number of cylinders filled and delivered and to running speeds.

Yet, again, it would be misleading simply to dwell on these traditional features. A notable aspect of the company is the absolutely strategic importance to the business of a group of employees who in many other businesses are seen as fairly marginal. For Air Products the drivers have been seen very much as part of the core. They have been the group who can make a reality of the possibility, mentioned at the outset of this case study, of bringing much of industry to a standstill. That is the negative point. The more positive aspect is that the company has seen these employees as absolutely central to their customer service strategy: they are the key point of interface with the customer and therefore they have in the past been bound ever tighter in to the company's affairs.

Unusually for a group of manual workers, for example, these drivers have individual performance appraisal. There is an extensive and sophisticated communications system, built around a network of 'key communicators', and there is an extensive set of benefits, including very advanced pension provision, which have given the company a reputation as a thoughtful and progressive employer. The value which it attaches to its relationship with its front-line workforce is indicated by its policy of insisting that all human resource managers should spend a period working on the delivery lorries, so that they have first-hand experience of working conditions.

Changing the industrial relations climate

As this relationship has evolved, the industrial relations climate in the company has been through an interesting transformation. In the 1970s the company had its full share of the acrimony and tension that typified relationships with strong and well-organised groups in inflationary times. Disputes were frequent and the atmosphere was frequently ill-tempered.

Looking back now, senior Air Products managers see that period as one in which the company struggled to find the right balance in its relationship with a unionised workforce whose performance was critical to the company's success. At times it went to great lengths to avoid confronting the workforce out of fear of the effects of industrial action, at other times it was determined to 'take' lengthy strike action over quite minor matters in order to establish a wider point. The overall effect of this process was a feeling of dissatisfaction – a sense that the company had won some important battles without winning the war.

Its strategy since then has been to work within the formal structures of the industrial relations system in order to build a closer relationship with employees as individuals and as a group. Cardinal features of this strategy have been communications, a very strong emphasis on safety, and an equally strong emphasis on fairness in its dealings with staff. Air Products is at pains to point out that the commercial benefit it gets from having improved staff performance and productivity could not have been achieved by a heavy-handed and unfair treatment of staff. The greater power that it has within the employment relationship has to be seen to be used fairly and responsibly.

This approach colours the company's attitude towards the trade unions who represent its employees. It has not sought to move against the unions. It has successfully sought to put its relationship with them onto a footing that it (and they) see as more constructive. It respects the full-time officials with whom it docs business – and they in turn are apt to hold the company up as something of a model employer. The union is seen as providing a clear and representative voice from the workforce and thus to provide information and feedback that the company would find it very hard to do without.

As far as Air Products is concerned its employees may be union members, but they are first and foremost company employees. It believes that this is also the attitude of the staff: that they see themselves as company employees who happen to take out union membership as an insurance policy. In so far as that has made them feel more secure in a time of great change the company has seen this as a net benefit. It has therefore been quite happy to maintain the structures and trappings of a traditional industrial relations system but to work within it to change the content of the relationship, and the climate in which it is conducted. That said, the situation is an evolving one. This is a highly competitive sector and the company's employee relations strategy is under constant review. Further changes are likely as the company seeks to maintain its position on costs. Whatever steps it takes, however, it is likely to continue to seek to maintain a close relationship with its employees and their representatives.

CHAPTER 8

What Future for Trade Unions?

INTRODUCTION

The starting point of this chapter is that the frequently (and rhetorically posed) question 'do unions have a future?' is no longer an interesting one. Their imminent demise has been so frequently predicted over the last decade and a half that it really is time to move on. After all it seems reasonable to assume that any organisations that can come through the non-stop battering that trade unions have encountered since 1979, with the walls of the house still standing and the roof more or less intact, will survive in some shape and size at least for the rest of our working lives.

The interesting questions then, and the ones that this chapter sets out to explore, are just what that shape and size will be. Not, therefore, *whether* trade unions have a future, but *what* their future is likely to be.

More positively: what factors, strategies or features will make for a *successful* trade union. Will more effective unions produce an expansion in trade union*ism*, or are we looking at a zero-sum game – one in which 'market share trade unionism' flourishes as unions compete to improve their share of a declining whole?

To shed some light on these and related questions the chapter first looks at the current state of unions as organisations and analyses exactly what success and failure means for them. We then review some of the main approaches that trade unions are currently taking to try to strengthen their position and assess the extent to which they are likely to meet the conditions for success. Some alternative approaches are suggested that revolve around establishing a greater degree of clarity about a union's fundamental purpose and business objectives. The final section of the chapter looks at how a business would try and turn itself around if it faced the sort of pressures faced by trade unions and the extent to which unions could apply some of these business processes and techniques in order better to face the future.

THE STATE OF THE UNIONS

In Chapter 5 we saw some of the data that charts the relative decline of the British trade union movement in the tough climate of the 1980s and 1990s. Among the key indicators of that decline are the following:

- Total trade union membership down from 13 million in 1979 to 8.5 million in 1993.
- Union density – total membership as a proportion of the civilian workforce in employment – down from 53 per cent in 1979 to 37 per cent in 1990.
- The proportion of the workforce covered by collective agreements down from over 55 per cent in 1983 to just 40 per cent in 1994.

To add to this picture, the pattern of union membership that remains indicates a vulnerability to further decline. For example, all of the industries where union density was above 50 per cent in 1993 were those where employment was largely or wholly in the public sector – or in industries, such as telecommunications, which used to be in the public sector. This means that many of the heartland areas of trade union membership are going to experience strong challenges in the coming years: from employment rationalisation and policy changes following privatisation; or from the contracting out of work to often non-union organisations; or, in the case of education and health (the sectors with the highest trade union density of all) from the fragmentation of employment relationships as local education authorities give way to locally managed and grant-maintained schools, and health authorities to self-governing hospital trusts.

In other words, it is not difficult to paint a picture of continuing decline in trade union membership, and in the standing and weight of the trade union presence in the economy. The more difficult question is, against that backdrop, what does it take for a union to succeed?

DEFINING SUCCESS AND FAILURE

One difficulty here is in finding reliable and unambiguous yardsticks with which to measure union success or failure. Membership size is bound to come into the equation, as is the proportion of the work group concerned represented by that membership. This cannot be the whole story, however, since it is possible to think of plenty of examples of *effective* trade unions that are neither particularly big (the mineworkers' union in the 1970s comes to mind) nor with particularly high membership density (this has often been the case in the construction industry for example).

Changes in either size, density or coverage of collective bargaining will, of course, feature in the picture, but there is also clearly something else in here which is about power or potency. The difficulty about this dimension, however, is that it is notoriously difficult to define in measurable terms. Is a high incidence of strike action, for example, a sign of union success or of failure? It will certainly serve as a good proxy for the militancy of a union, but it is quite possible to argue that the measure of a union's real strength is that it rarely, if ever, has to resort to strike action. This argument has been applied for example to the Electrical Power Engineers Association (part of the Engineers and Managers Association) whose members control the operation of power stations and are in a position of such enormous strategic strength that they have been able to achieve many of their goals without ever really having to flex their collective muscles.

Does power equate automatically with success, however? There seems to be something unsatisfactory in an argument that deems that, because a particular work group – say power station managers – have great industrial power due to the nature of their role, their union will by definition be more successful than, say, a union like Unison, which represents groups such as school dinner ladies and care assistants.

As well as the outward signs of potency, therefore, the concept of success for a trade union seems to embrace also some measure of the *results* of their activities – their value added, whether in terms of the 'mark up' of union members' wages over those of their non-union equivalents, the degree of control exercised over employment procedures, the shape of the wages/employment trade-off or the contribution made to the employer's performance – and of the way in which the union is *managed* as an organisation in its own right. This latter dimension has to take account of the fact that trade unions are both business organisations – with staff to pay, funds to manage and services to provide – and representative organisations, with strong internal political structures and processes designed to enable members to articulate policy demands and to hold officials to account for the success and energy with which they have pursued them.

The balance here is all important. Some of the unions that were apparently most successful in the 1980s in conventional business (ie financial) terms were so because they were relatively inactive, or because they represented memberships that were dwindling as a result of industrial restructuring. Equally, unions which energetically rode into battle in pursuit of over-ambitious membership or leadership demands sometimes did lasting damage to the fabric and solvency of their organisations.

So, the process of defining success and failure for a trade union faces us with an apparently complicated picture to piece together. We are helped in this, however, by a very useful model from a research team at the London Business School, led by Professor Paul Willman.[1] The model is illustrated in Figure 8.1. It shows unions operating in two 'marketplaces', of employers and members respectively.

The left hand boxes show what it is that unions have to offer to their potential customers. For employers the 'products' which might appeal are the provision of a reliable channel for the voice of their employees – very much in the way discussed in Chapter 6 – and/or some influence over the supply of skills to the organisation. This might take the form of some positive contribution to the development of new skills by the workforce, (as offered for example by the engineering and electricians' union), or it may reflect a partial monopoly of key skills on the part of a particular union (as was the case in the printing industry, for example).

For members and potential members there are three areas in which a union might be able to make a successful appeal. The first is the provision of *collective* services: the classic union role of negotiating collectively with an employer or group of employers in order to reach an agreement regulating terms and conditions of employment.

The second category of *semi-collective* services represents an area of support that the union can make available to an individual because of the existence of some collective arrangement. A good example might be the representation of a member with a grievance, or one who is being disciplined, using the provisions of a collectively-agreed grievance or disciplinary procedure. It is in other words about the individual interpretation and application of the terms of a collective agreement.

The Twin Markets for Trade Unions

Unions operate in two 'markets' and need 'products' that satisfy both employers and members

In each market, unions have key objectives . . .

. . . which provide key outcomes

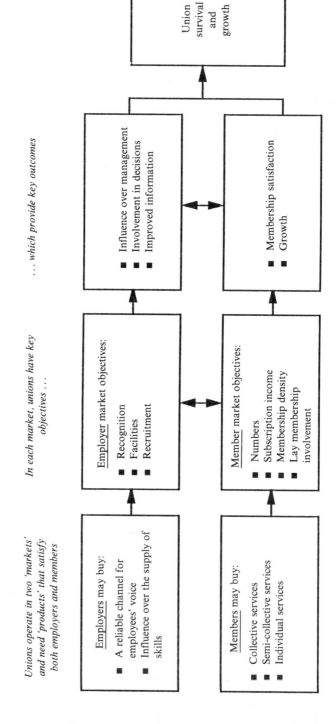

Employers may buy:

- A reliable channel for employees' voice
- Influence over the supply of skills

Employer market objectives:

- Recognition
- Facilities
- Recruitment

Influence over management
- Involvement in decisions
- Improved information

Members may buy:

- Collective services
- Semi-collective services
- Individual services

Member market objectives:

- Numbers
- Subscription income
- Membership density
- Lay membership involvement

Membership satisfaction
- Growth

Union survival and growth

Figure 8.1   The twin markets for trade unions

Source: William, P, et al (1993) Union Business

Third, there is the category of *individual* services – benefits that come from union membership, irrespective of the existence or otherwise of agreements with employers. Included here are both the traditional 'Friendly Society' benefits (accident benefit, sickness support, and so on) as well as the more modern benefits – such as cheap insurance, holiday deals, financial services etc – for which the union acts as a broker, using the size and profile of its membership to negotiate special discounts from suppliers. A key point here is that the more that a union is drawn away from a focus on the provision of collective services and into the semi-collective and individual categories, the more steeply the per capita cost of servicing its membership takes off.

The model goes on to summarise the key business objectives that a trade union will need to pursue in each market – and the inter-relationships between them. Thus, for example, a major requirement in the employer market is to secure the *infrastructure* that will enable it to operate effectively. Recognition agreements bring a licence to operate within the organisation and a framework of procedural agreements enabling the union to represent its members there. Facilities granted to workplace representatives – in the form of paid time off for union activities, office space, access to telephones and photocopiers etc, make a reality of the union's presence in the organisation. And agreement by the employer to collect union subscriptions at source by deducting them from pay packets and transferring the money to the union, and to tell new staff that the company has a positive (or at least a non-hostile) attitude towards trade union membership mean in effect that the employer undertakes the core activities of recruitment and income collection for the union.

What the union is doing through the pursuit of these employer market objectives is to seek to generate and then maximise an employer *subsidy* to cover a large part of the operating costs of trade unionism. The scale of that subsidy can be gauged by the following points:

■ It is estimated that some 90 per cent of the subscription income of the two biggest general trade unions – the TGWU and the GMB – has been collected by check-off arrangements: in other words, by employers.
■ Three-quarters of union members have paid their subscriptions by check-off.

Without this subsidy the union is forced, for example, to shift away from an organisational model based upon an extensive network of employer-subsidised lay officials towards one that relies on a smaller number of much more costly full-time officials. Crucially the impact of this and similar developments will mean that the union is forced to raise subscription levels, thereby making its position uncompetitive *vis à vis* other unions seeking to recruit in the same sector, and running the risk that the cost/benefit calculation in members' minds will come out against the advantages of continuing membership. As membership declines, the case for the employer continuing to provide recognition and facilities is weakened, and so a downward spiral sets in.

The interdependency between the two markets is shown in other ways. Thus, for example, a union may well find itself competing against other unions for recognition in the employer market: this was famously true in the case of the greenfield site, single union deals of the 1980s. In such cases the union will be trying to impress upon the employer the benefits that it can bring to the business. It will be mindful, however, that if it concentrates exclusively on this side of the system, to the point where it gains a reputation as a 'sweetheart' union, it will undermine its ability to deliver anything of substance in respect of the influence and involvement summarised in the top right-hand box in Figure 8.1, and will thereby weaken its ability to operate in the member market. The risk is that after a while its presence in the organisation will be that of an empty shell – all form and little substance – and that after a while the employer will feel no hesitation in simply brushing it aside.

MANAGING THE TRADE UNION PORTFOLIO

This 'two market' model then is a useful framework. It does not pretend to explain or predict how unions will behave, and it has very little to say about a union's internal political and governmental life. What it does provide, however, is something that fits our purposes extremely well: a framework with which to judge the chances of particular strategies and approaches achieving the basic goal of union survival and growth, which is the ultimate measure of success or failure.

At the heart of this framework is an important truth about trade unions. They are portfolios of very different membership groups, with a strong element of cross-subsidy between them, rather like multi-divisional companies. And just as with a multi-divisional company, success with a trade union depends upon the effective management of the portfolio as a whole, and of the successful exploitation of any potential synergies between the component elements of the portfolio.

The depiction of the membership market in the London Business School model shows members paying individual subscriptions in exchange for particular packages of collective, semi-collective and individual services. In balance sheet terms, however, the position of different groups of members typically will vary enormously. In settled, stable areas of organisation, marked by well-developed structures and facilities, union revenues will generally exceed the costs of servicing and maintaining the group of members concerned. The major exception will be at times of industrial action when the union will have to subsidise members' wages from strike funds.

In less-settled, relatively unorganised areas, the position is reversed. Here the cost of providing trade union services exceeds the revenue available from members (and from employer subsidy). This is either because the union concerned is trying competitively to enter a new area of employment – one of the key findings of the London Business School research is that attempts at competitive recruitment pose the major threat to a union's financial position – or because the absence of well-developed collective bargaining arrangements means that the union is drawn into the much more expensive business of providing individual servicing to a dispersed and heterogeneous membership group.

Thus, union attempts to organise non-union areas of employment are funded by the surplus generated by long-standing groups of members. Another way of looking at it is that it is the subsidy provided by unionised employers that finances recruitment drives and union activities in the non-union sector. As Willman *et al*[2] point out, 'The essence of collective action is that it involves cross-subsidy'. As they go on to demonstrate, however, union rule books and recruitment literature tend to stay silent on this matter. The appeal is made directly to the potential member in terms of what the union can do to help *them* as an individual or as a member of a tightly-defined employment group, as if they were self-contained units who would always tend to get more out of belonging to a union than they put into it; whereas in fact they are joining a portfolio organisation in which the chances are that they will be subsidising the membership benefits of others.

A question of fundamental importance for the future therefore is whether such a model can survive. Everything that we have seen so far in this book suggests that this process of cross-subsidy which has enabled British trade unionism to survive will increasingly come under attack from three sources:

1.   The growing reluctance of employers – even those who continue to recognise trade unions – to continue to subsidise their activities on the scale of the past. (The latest legislation requiring periodic membership reaffirmation by ballot of 'check-off' arrangements will add greatly to this pressure.)
2.   The growing size of the non-union sector, and the growing number of employment grievances within it, which will put up the cost and therefore the cross-subsidy needed for unions to try to enter and operate effectively in this sector.
3.   The increasing reluctance of individual trade union members to cross-subsidise the servicing of other groups due to the growing emphasis on, and identification with, the circumstances of their individual employer, the dismantling of many of the cross-industry structures that previously produced some identity of interest with other groups of workers, and the general, society-wide trend towards a more individualistic and less solidaristic culture.

The results of their analysis of trends in the financial, membership and organisational position of a number of trade unions in the 1980s led Professor Willman and his colleagues to conclude that the twin conditions for union success in the future would continue to be the existence or creation of what they termed 'a defensible job territory' (ie one which among other things would not be subject to debilitating inter-union competition) together with the pursuit of a very businesslike and professional approach towards membership service provision and the management of the union's resources. They also concluded that the portfolio model of organisation was the only effective form for the expansion of trade unionism, and that just as employer support and subsidy had underpinned the current pattern of activity so too it would be needed in order to underpin its expansion.

We will return to this point later in the chapter because if our earlier contention is true that the prospects of such employer support are *diminishing* rather than growing, then it is crucial to ask whether other bases are available for an expansion of unions and of trade unionism as a whole or whether, alternatively, we are left with 'market share unionism' in which the success of one union can only be at the expense of another.

First, however, we will take a look at some of the approaches that some of the major trade unions have taken in recent years towards trying to secure their futures in the wake of the decline in union fortunes of the 1980s. In doing this we will be trying to move closer to the answer to two questions:

1. How do these approaches measure up to the requirements of the 'two market model' that we looked at above – and, in particular, to what extent have they succeeded in providing unions with a defensible job territory?
2. Do they provide the basis for a general expansion in trade unionism, or are they manifestations of zero-sum, market-share trade unionism?

UNION STRATEGIES FOR HARD TIMES

It is possible to identify three major separate approaches that unions have taken in response to the cold climate of the last decade and a half. We shall look at these in turn (bearing in mind as we do that individual unions may well have followed more than one strategy at different times – or even at the same time!). The strategies are, respectively, *recruiting* in the new areas of employment, *merger* between union organisations, and appealing to employers as *partners in change*. We find as we examine them that they do touch on the main priority areas for unions – job territory, cost levels, and responding to employers' agendas. We also raise serious doubts about the effectiveness with which these strategies have been pursued to date.

Reaching out to the new labour force

A major theme of the late 1980s was the realisation by the big general unions that their disproportionate presence among manual, male workers in large scale manufacturing industries represented a long-term threat to the survival of their membership base. Part of the response to this realisation (notably by the TGWU and the GMB, but also by the shop workers union USDAW) was to launch programmes of recruitment and associated activities designed to make big inroads into the unorganised sectors.

The main target areas were service sector industries characterised by more flexible forms of employment – and in particular by a high incidence of part-time and temporary working – predominantly female workforces, a high incidence of ethnic minority employment, and low pay. The hotel and catering trade, retail industries and contract cleaning were among the major targets.

Typically, the principal components of this approach were the following:

■ A targeted recruitment drive, with full-time officers and key lay activists being given designated 'prospects' to go after, a reallocation of responsibilities so that less time and resource was correspondingly put into the servicing of established groups of members, and some form of incentive or reward scheme to support the achievement of recruitment targets.

■ An attempt to brush up the image of the union so as to give it an appeal to the 'new' workforce who hitherto may have associated the unions with a more established workforce with whom they appeared to have little in common and who often regarded their work as falling outside the category of 'proper jobs'. Often this process went far beyond a superficial concern with image and produced substantive changes in, for example, the number of women and ethnic minority officials, and in the representative structure of the union – making it much easier for these new groups of members to have an effective voice within the union.

■ The identification of specific industrial and employment issues of particular concern to the targets of the recruitment campaign. Examples included sex bias in employment contracts, racial discrimination, inadequate protection against accidents at work and so on. Linked to this was a general political campaign in favour of a new set of individual employment rights, which would enable unions to position themselves as the enforcement arm for vulnerable groups of workers.

■ A restructuring of the union's subscription and benefit package so as to make it more relevant to the groups concerned. This might, for example, include putting a greater emphasis on the provision of legal and related advisory services and less on the more traditional friendly society benefits. It might also entail providing a greater range of individual benefits and services not linked to the workplace or to the existence of a collective agreement. Cheap insurance, special shopping discounts or cheap deals on holidays have all featured in union campaigns.

In terms of the London Business School model then this represented a major move away from the provision of collective services towards individual services and semi-collective services predicated on the assumption of a new legal framework of enforceable rights.

How should we draw up the balance sheet of this type of strategy? In its favour is the simple point that in seeking to organise the growing periphery of the labour market the general unions have been acting out their main historical role. The 'flexible' workforces in the hotel and cleaning trades are the exact present day counterpart of the casualised dock labourers and unskilled operatives whom the general unions came into existence to organise one hundred years ago. Moreover, in seeking to put, as it were, a floor underneath the terms and conditions set in the flexible part of the labour market, these unions have from their point of view been trying to limit the impact of deregulation on workers in the organised sector.

The problem is that as a strategy it does not seem to have been very successful – at least as measured in the bottom line of membership growth. The latest annual returns for example show the GMB's membership declining yet again by over 60,000, or 7 per cent.

Three things seem to have gone wrong. First, the force of the organising attempts of unions in the non-unionised private sector seems to have been insufficient to overcome the resistance of employers. Second, some of the unions concerned may have underestimated the extent of the transformation in their own organisations and cultures required to turn themselves from predominantly servicing bodies for essentially stable and passive groups of members into energetic champions of expansion. In this respect also it may just be that internal resistance to the additional degree of cross-subsidy from 'insider' groups involved in making this shift proved too strong.

Third, it may be that the offering that unions could put forward in these areas of employment have lacked conviction. Certainly those features of it that were predicated on major changes in employment rights were sunk by the 1992 General Election – and the Social Chapter of the Maastricht Treaty is clearly going to provide no effective substitute, at least in the UK.

Within the present and foreseeable legislative and economic framework the difficulty for trade unions is this. Where they can gain recognition from employers in the 'new' sectors, their ability to deliver major improvements in terms and conditions is very constrained in what are by and large low-margin, cost-competitive parts of the low productivity tail of the British economy. Where they are not recognised, their ability to offer really attractive individual services is limited by the low subscription levels which competitive trade unionism forces upon them and by the internal political constraints on massive cross-subsidy from members who derive only collective services from the union.

Getting together

A second response to the years of decline has been a wave of trade union mergers that have quite redrawn the map and pecking order of union representation. The country's largest union is now also its newest: Unison, formed in 1993 from a merger of NALGO, the local government white collar union, NUPE, its blue collar counterpart, and COHSE, the health workers' union. The two biggest and longest standing craft-based unions – the Engineers and the Electricians – have come together in the new AEEU. And the GMB, having merged with a sizable white collar union, APEX, and with a number of small trade-based bodies, for example in the textiles industry, is now actively pursuing the ultimate trade union merger – with the Transport and General Workers Union – that would create the 'one big union' of nineteenth-century labour dreams.

Whereas the motivation for the recruitment strategies described above has been primarily the expansion of trade unionism into virgin territory, the rationale for the merger strategy has been much more defensive. Principally it has been concerned with the consolidation of union membership within a unionised sector, and the rationalisation of union resources through the achievement of economies of scale.

Thus, for example, the GMB/APEX merger was pursued in part because it was realised that the two unions had quite complementary membership patterns. In many workplaces the GMB held negotiating rights for hourly-paid workers but non-manual staff were unorganised. Equally, APEX were represented in a number of establishments where manual workers were unorganised. The strategy was therefore to gain leverage from these respective positions in order to 'infill' the total membership of the merged union, thus creating larger and easier to service groups of members.

Not all mergers have had the same degree of industrial logic – sometimes owing more to political alignments than to business sense. In extreme cases (and the ill-fated marriage of the engineering union in the 1960s with the draughtsmen's union was *the* extreme case) unsuccessful mergers can paralyse a trade union just as much as they can a conglomerate company. Indeed, in the trade union world as much as in the business world, mergers can fail because of clashes of culture or of personalities. Nevertheless, in terms of the general industrial relations scene, it is clear that the 1990s will be the decade of the creation of the 'super union'.

As well as the case for consolidation and rationalisation of resources mentioned above, there are two related reasons for this trade union merger mania. The first is that sometimes a carefully chosen merger partner can give credibility to a recruitment drive by giving a union a foothold in a new sector. The second is that a merger can sometimes ease the way to cross-subsidisation within a union by filling the space between what would otherwise be two very distant groups with little or no sense of common purpose.

In this respect therefore the strategy can meet the London Business School's prescription for trade union success: the creation of a defensible job territory plus a cost effective organisation. It might, in some circumstances, appeal to employers by reducing the number of unions with which they have to deal. Equally, in other circumstances, it might deter an employer by bringing into the workplace, through the merger, a union with which it has not chosen voluntarily to do business. It may similarly dismay an established group of members if they feel that merger will detract from a union identity with which they feel a particularly strong affinity. In most cases, however, this is unlikely to be the reaction. Indifference or a mild interest in the modernised services or benefits that accompany the merger are more commonplace.

The underlying fact about the merger strategy as a trade union response to hard times, however, is that it represents 'market share' trade unionism pure and simple. It is not about pushing out the frontiers of trade union organisation – indeed it is a strategy that is often consciously chosen as an alternative: the consolidation of membership volume in more cost-effective patterns within the existing boundaries of trade union organisation. A strategy, in other words, of managed decline.

Particularly in the public sector (and in local government especially), this strategy has been associated with another feature of managed decline. The focus of much union activity has been the defensive struggle of trying to protect procedural gains made in an earlier period, even though the scope for negotiating improvements in terms and conditions through these procedures has been minimal. The rationale here has partly been to secure the institutional survival of the union in the hope of better days ahead.

Behind this, however, has been a more deliberate – indeed uncompromising - stance of posing the highly regulated and codified procedures of a public sector collective agreement as an alternative, and in fact a superior model to the new, more managerial and flexible way of doing business in these sectors. Thus what looks like red tape and inflexibility to a town hall manager trying to get a job done in a hurry or needing to reconcile growing local demands for services with centrally-dictated resource cuts, is defended by a Unison rep as a fairer, more considered and inherently better way of going about things.

This strategy has not been unsuccessful, leaving most parts of the public sector that have not been privatised or contracted out with frameworks of employment practice regulation that owe much more to the 1970s than to the 1980s or 1990s. The results can be strange. It can lead, for example, to the recruitment of staff through an equal opportunities interviewing procedure of great sophistication, and with job share arrangements that are wholly to the employee's advantage, into a workplace bereft of even the basic facilities needed to do the job, an atmosphere of gloom and demotivation and pay levels that are far below any private sector comparator.

Equally perversely the union can find itself preparing to fight to its dying breath to protect part of an agreement that it never really liked in the first place but which it feels it now must defend simply because it *is* part of the collective agreement and it is from the agreement that the union derives its legitimacy. Thus it is, for example, that we find unions with radically egalitarian policy stances protecting job evaluation systems and grade structures that perpetuate workplace relationships that are hierarchical and disempowering.

Overall, a key point about merger as a strategy for union survival is that it is a very inwardly-driven approach. It is a union issue, rather than a union *member* issue. It is not usually rooted primarily in a consideration of what members want, or of how the service provided to them can be improved. Indeed, not surprisingly, most trade union members remain sublimely indifferent to the formal structure of their union   as witnessed by the very low participation in ballots of members called to approve merger proposals.

There are two other concluding observations to be made about the merger strategy. The first is that there is serious room to doubt whether the supposed economies of scale which drive it are ever realised in practice. Many mergers have not resulted in improvements in per capita administration costs. The energy that goes into constructing the merged conglomerate is rarely applied to the search for efficiency gains within the new entity. The political trading which is often required in order to cajole key interest groups into partnership can have an expensive legacy. Dual structures are maintained, individuals remain in posts for which there is little justification, there is duplication rather than rationalisation.

The creation of Unison has demonstrated many of these features. The earlier merger between the GMWU and the Boilermakers was quite a vivid case in point. A set of political and administrative compromises locked costs into the merged structure. Separate rulebooks were maintained, officer-to-member ratios were maintained and the merged GMBU inherited the huge litigation costs for industrial injuries that had built up in the shipbuilding industry.

Second, it is notable that 'merger mania' should have broken out in the union world at the very time when it has been largely discredited as a commercial business strategy. In the business world the focus has been on 'unbundling', on the creation of a focus around the needs of tightly-defined groups of customers, on organisation around process, rather than around conglomeration. In later sections of this chapter we examine the relevance of these developments for unions themselves.

Enterprise trade unionism

The third broad strategy which unions have followed in response to the cold climate of the 1980s and 1990s has been aimed squarely at the employer market. 'Enterprise unionism' seeks to present the union as a partner in managing change in the workplace. Its antecedents are the productivity councils and agreements of the war years and the post war period, and it draws some inspiration from the 'business unionism' of the US.

The clearest expression of this approach lay in the competitive pitches that several unions made towards employers seeking to sign single union deals in the late 1980s. These deals – many of which were controversial at the time – are summarised in Chapter 5. In essence they were pre-membership agreements, establishing the union as part of the structure of the enterprise, one which in return for membership would be expected to contribute directly and constructively to the effective management of the enterprise. This might be in a passive sense, by refraining from practices and activities that were regarded as a trade union norm in other areas, or in a more active sense, by encouraging the adoption of team-working, problem solving and other techniques on the part of the workforce.

Outside the rather narrow realm of the single union deal other manifestations of enterprise unionism can be found. Some unions have taken important initiatives in the training field. The engineering union, for example, launched a pioneering programme of training in the skills associated with manufacturing robotics. The aim was both to help strengthen the skill base of its members and to impress upon employers the value of doing business with an organisation that could play a useful role in technological adaptation. In similar vein the electricians' union took to using its own training centre as a resource, available to firms that wanted to use it, to bring managers and workforce together to work on issues of competitive concern.

It is possible to cite instances where the pursuit of enterprise unionism has chimed with the attitude of an employer and a participative approach to change has resulted. The case of H&R Johnson, examined in Chapter 7, has some of these features. The adoption of Japanese-style working practices in Rover cars was marked by some very businesslike inputs from the trade unions there; so indeed was the development of the innovative Education and Development Assistance Programme (EDAP) employee development programme in Ford.

Overall, however, one is struck by the relative scarcity of examples of successful enterprise unionism in practice. This is for two reasons. First, the application of this approach by unions has been patchy. Even within individual unions there are disparities in the degree of application, often reflecting the federal and devolved nature of the organisations themselves.

Second, and more germane to the main theme of the book, it takes two to make a partnership and, by and large, employers have become increasingly uninterested in letting even a modern and 'businesslike' union into the inner circle of decision-making. This creates a strong contrast with some observed features of the US industrial scene, where labour relations is narrower in its base but often deeper in the degree of partnership.

Returning to the UK context then there are three concluding points to be made about the enterprise unionism strategy. First, it is not a widely-developed approach. Second, it is not a strategy that expands the boundaries of trade union organisation: it tends to be found in the industrial heartlands rather than at the frontiers. Third, however, it proceeds from a firm desire to understand and respond to employer concerns and priorities.

REINVENTING TRADE UNIONISM

Let us take a cool, businesslike look at the prospects for trade unionism in the light of this analysis. We have looked in some detail at recent developments and we have seen 'the coffin' – the prospect of continuing steep decline on present trends. We have tried to understand the messages from the marketplace and we have examined the chief strategies that have been adopted in the light of those messages. If we were looking at the business strategies of a group of companies how would we construct the balance sheet?

The proposition here is that there is a contrast between the clarity of the messages from the marketplace and the confusion that characterises the responses, and that this confusion is getting in the way of the development of a more effective trade unionism.

First the messages. On one side of the market the evidence is that employers want less contact and fewer dealings with trade unions, but that in so far as they are willing to do business it is a different sort of business. They want a clear focus on *their* particular circumstances rather than being seen as part of a wider undifferentiated industry or regional grouping. They want to deal with *their* employees on an agenda that they lead and which integrates with their business strategies. They are happier dealing with representatives from within the organisation and less willing to deal with union officials from outside. Increasingly they want a single point of contact with trade unions and greatly prefer dealing with an organisation that shares their territory: in short they want something that is as close as possible to a company union and are impatient with anything that falls far short of one.

Employees too have developed a much more individualistic focus. Individualism is the key element in modern employee relations and its growth in the past decade has transformed the scene. As it has grown so too have unions set out to oppose it, and in doing so they have quite misread the aspirations of their members and potential members. As a recent Fabian pamphlet put it:[3]

> For many employees now, big monolithic collective unions are part of their past, like big monolithic Labour, or big councils, or renting their homes, or living in inner city areas. Like Labour, the unions are seen as mechanisms for holding people back, for restricting individual improvement and individual achievement, rather than empowering them. For their own good, unions in Britain must move away from being associated with failure – failed employment relationships in failed industries – and must instead try to associate themselves with success: successful employees, successful employee relations, successful employers.

The argument of the authors was that more than ever before the reasons for joining trade unions were instrumental and individualistic – 'what's in it for me?' In support of this they cited research undertaken for the public service union NUPE, which showed that the key reasons for joining hinged on a very individualistic agenda. Advice on discipline, legal assistance, advice on grievances all came in higher than pay negotiation and far higher than a solidaristic commitment to collectivist trade unionism.

Against the clarity of these messages from their respective marketplaces the responses of unions seem to lack focus. It is as if they have been trying to sustain an unrealistic range of conflicting roles:

- *Champion:* lifting the floor of the labour market to improve minimum pay and standards.
- *Equaliser:* attempting to eradicate differentials that are based on gender, race or location.
- *Ladder:* enhancing skill development and promotion opportunities.
- *Regulator:* imposing or defending workplace rules that limit managerial license to act.
- *Membership club:* providing a new range of financial and other services.

The confusion is made worse by the fact that different unions are trying to pursue a number of these different roles simultaneously.

So the issue is not that all unions need to be forced into one restrictive role or structure. Rather it is that like all successful businesses they need to ask themselves what business they are in, and, for trade unionism to flourish as a whole, they need to do this within a process from which individual unions can learn and gain, so that it doesn't simply become a squabble over the remains.

In other words, like many businesses and indeed whole sectors, unions face the challenge of re-engineering – or reinventing – themselves. And there are some sound lessons from successful business practice that unions could draw upon in this process. Pulling these together we can envisage a five-stage process which could lead to the emergence of a greatly-strengthened trade union movement in the UK.

Determine the core competencies

What are unions uniquely good at? What is it that they can do that other agencies cannot do better? What, in the jargon, is their core competence? A firm understanding of the answer to this question is the first stage in the re-engineering process.

The answer does not lie in the provision of financial services or other 'club' type benefits. It is not realistic to think that even a large union can compete with the major financial or commercial institutions. It may have the distribution channels but it has no product development capability; it has to buy in other people's products and it carries the overhead cost of its own administrative and representative structures. Similarly it is not well equipped to provide an all-purpose professional, legal, accounting or other business service. At the other end of the spectrum unions do not have the edge in terms of the provision of general policy advice – whether on the overall state of the economy, the defence of the nation or the situation in Gaza (on all of which subjects many unions spend valuable resources and make frequent pronouncements).

Instead the core competence of unions lies in the articulation and handling of issues that spring directly out of working life. Better than any other organisation, a union at its best is able to bring together its representative and administrative halves in a powerful way to unlock issues and bring them to the surface, to represent particular employees or groups of employees – giving them specialist support where needed – to articulate the policy implications of that issue and to pursue a generalised remedy or resolution of it. This is true whether the issue is one of pay, of discrimination, of unfair or vindictive treatment, of unsafe or unhealthy working conditions or the introduction of new management techniques or working technologies. The unique competence of a union therefore is around representation on the one hand and problem solving and prevention on the other.

We think most readily of these activities in terms of the services that a union provides to members whose employment is stable in a particular location. In principle, however, it is possible to project this on to the more mobile world of 'portfolio employment' described by Charles Handy[4] (although it is necessary to bear in mind that union membership is often one of the things that such workers psychologically 'leave behind' when they make the transition into the more mobile economy). That said, as an increasing number of people travel through a working lifetime composed of different types of employment contract, and with a greater emphasis on the self management of careers, an organisation that could travel with them on that journey, broking solutions to problems concerning contracts, pensions, training needs and so on would greatly ease what would otherwise be a complex and time-consuming set of worries.

Ask the people

The problem, as Philip Bassett put it in his Fabian pamphlet, is that there has been 'quite simply a collapse in demand for the core product that unions have traditionally offered to their twin markets – collectivism enshrined most obviously in collective bargaining'.[5]

Earlier in this section we charted the factors that lay behind this slump in demand. By and large, unions have not really picked this message up and have continued to behave as if their fundamental purpose in life will continue to be the provision of collective bargaining. Certainly they continue to devote a disproportionately high level of resources to the servicing of collective bargaining rather than to the pursuit of the growing individualistic agenda. But unions are private sector organisations in the business of providing services; it is high time they listened more closely to how, in the changed employment markets of the 1990s, people are describing their needs.

A summary of needs in the employee market would include the following:

- Advice and assistance on the negotiation of *individual contracts*. These are an increasingly common feature of the employment scene and are often presented to employees in a 'take it or leave it' fashion.
- *Individual representation*. This need can arise in respect of traditional concerns such as disciplinary or grievance hearings, or industrial tribunals. It can also arise in cases of 'whistle blowing' – where an individual feels a moral imperative to break the rules in order to reveal a perceived hidden abuse. The growth in performance appraisal systems has added a new dimension as well.
- *Personal development*. Previous chapters have emphasised the growing importance attached to continuous skill development in the era of HRM. Yet many employees are short of information about possible sources of appropriate training and feel a lack of support in choosing the right development path.
- *Pensions advice*. With the growth of personal pensions and increasing mobility between jobs, more and more people feel in need of good advice on the value of their pensions. At the same time the trend towards tie-ups between banks, insurance companies and other financial institutions has led to more people feeling suspicious about the availability of genuinely independent advice. Recent spectacular cases of abuse – notably the Maxwell case – and the more insidious stream of regular revelations of inefficiency and bad value in the pensions industry have increased the demand for a trustworthy service in this area.
- *Health and safety support*. The explosive growth in the use of new office and factory technologies has transformed the working environment for many – taking them into situations where previous experience gives no guide to safe and healthy working practices. The growth in outworking ('telecommuting' in its extreme form) is taking increasing numbers of people into more isolated workplaces where advice and guidance is less available, and where the previously simple physical boundary between work and home life no longer exists.

All of these, and similar, demands are likely to grow around a declining but still significant core of demand for more traditional collective bargaining representation.

From the employer market comes a smaller but challenging set of demands:

- *Strengthening the human resource*. Human skills and talents increasingly provide the competitive edge, but firms often feel that they haven't got all the development levers in their hands. Can a union help build the skills of a workforce and sharpen the contribution made to quality programmes etc?

■ *Improving communications and commitment.* With the growing concern to build the commitment of the workforce to the enterprise's success can a union help to get messages travelling faster around the organisation and be more clearly understood?

■ *Managing the flexible workforce.* Employment flexibility brings headaches as well as cost savings – a wider range of contracts to manage, more staff to find, different management styles to adopt and so on. Can a union present itself as a partner, a sort of facilities manager on the employment front, to help manage this complex world more effectively?

Redesign the service offerings

In the light of these market demands it is possible to see the way in which unions could redesign their service offerings around the core competencies identified above. Here by way of illustration are four 'bundles' of service offering for a hypothetical union. This is not an exhaustive set and, as the Evaluation section which follows makes clear, there are some significant tensions and points of choice within and between the bundles. However, for illustrative purposes they will serve.

Representation and advice service

The aim here is to provide a service that is not dependent on the existence of a collective agreement and its corresponding rights and facilities. The service might have three levels. A telephone help line would provide quick and reliable answers to basic employment issues. (The demand for this is indicated by the many thousands of queries on employment matters that are handled each year by Citizens Advice Bureaux, and also by the growing use by employees of lawyers for similar issues.) At the next level more complex queries concerning contractual issues, or health and safety or employment rights would be handled by drawing on the detailed expertise that at present is often kept locked up in the heads or files of lay representatives and full-time officers.

If matters came to a head and a member needed professional representation – whether in order to send a warning letter or to appear at a tribunal hearing – this would be provided by the union's specialists. It is credible to offer this service even in the absence of formal representation rights since very few organisations will actually refuse to see someone who is acting on behalf of an employee – especially someone wearing a solicitor's hat.

Getting change to stick

At the moment a manager who wants to take a union along in the introduction of a new technique – total quality, say, or just-in-time management, or MRP, or process re-engineering – is probably in for a thin time. He may ask for constructive comment and input but the chances are that he won't get it, not through malevolence but through lack of knowledge on the union side. After a while the manager will give this up as a waste of time and will get on with the change regardless: the marginalisation of the union continues apace.

This is very frustrating because the chances are that somewhere within its network the union's membership has experience and understanding of the change issues that could add real value to the firm in question. A local representative in another firm has seen the same new process introduced in another workplace and has got strong and well informed views on how work groups could be better structured around it. An official has heard from another union – perhaps an overseas one – about the changes in management practice and skills that have been introduced elsewhere in order to get the best value out of the change. Someone in the research department produced a really good paper on leading-edge experience with the new technique – but it has been lying unread at the bottom of another official's briefcase for the last fortnight. Unions by and large are very bad at pooling their internal knowledge and experience and making it easily available in value-adding form at the sharp end.

The idea for this service offering then is to change this state of affairs – to build a readily-accessible information service that puts the organisation's accumulated experience in the hands of those who most need it now. In addition the union going down this path would take a much more flexible approach to the deployment of its people. If somebody gained real experience and insights about overcoming the problems connected with the introduction of a particular process or technique, rather than locking them into servicing a particular firm or area, they would be seen as a union-wide resource. Their brief would be to take the following stance with an employer. 'You want to introduce total quality management. Four out of five TQ programmes fail outright on the people side: because they do not produce lasting changes in behaviour. Changes in behaviour require changes in work organisation, responsibility levels, management practices and so on. I know which changes are most likely to get results: let's talk.'

Working lifetime partnership

This service offering would be designed to run alongside the career of a mobile worker – someone whose working lifetime spanned a number of organisations (some unionised, most not), took in a couple of changes in occupational direction and included spells of part-time work and self employment.

The idea behind the offering would be to provide a one-stop shop through which such workers can regularly update and refine the various packages of pension, taxation, insurance, training and contract advice and support for which at present he or she needs to go shopping laboriously in a range of different markets. The union would, in other words, offer itself as a sort of 'super broker' constantly looking for the best value and innovative products and services on offer in the whole employment-related field and packaging them up in ways that are designed around specific employment scenarios.

Through this service a union could also meet the demand for support in the negotiation of personal contracts. Most of the contracts offered to individuals are in reality marginally-modified versions of a standard document. What is individual about an individual contract is often little more than the employee's name. However, for the employee who does not necessarily know that this is the case it can be a daunting document, and the idea that it is open to him or her to propose amendments and to withhold signature until he or she has agreed the content is quite alien. It would therefore be a powerful move for a union to offer an employee, through the creation of a straightforward database of optional clauses backed up by relevant argumentation, the chance to move from the position of supplicant to that of a full partner in an individual negotiation.

Flexible friend

This illustrative offering is at the whacky end of the spectrum but it is worth considering because it could get unions into the game in a large slice of the labour market where currently they are in retreat or banging their heads against a wall trying to gain entry. It is based upon the premise that the business of managing a more flexible labour market is, from the employer's point of view, a pain and therefore that any help they can receive may be gratefully received.

In effect the union would present itself to the employer as the contracting supplier of its labour force – transforming its membership list into a sort of employment register. In this respect the approach would draw on the old tradition of a union 'hiring hall', developed in response to earlier periods of casualisation. The difference would be however that this new offering would include a commitment to improve the quality of labour, rather as modern approaches to facilities management seek to create a partnership between outsourcer and contractor, which leads to a mutually-beneficial improvement in the service provided. The stance of the union would be to say 'we will take on the hassle of providing you with the types of labour you want, when and where you want it. We'll agree a price, but the key to success lies not in minimising the short term price of labour but in improving its long term quality. You'll pay more for our labour but (a) you'll avoid a lot of the pain in organising its supply and (b) you'll be part of a partnership which is involved in training and developing the workforce so that it can make a progressively stronger contribution to your business. Union labour is better quality labour.'

Evaluation

Not all of these service offerings will make sense for all unions at all times in all parts of the labour market. Indeed for unions for whom the maintenance of effective, employer-subsidised collective bargaining is a realistic possibility this is always going to be the favoured option. Since, however, the argument of this book is that the scope for this is going to be continually eroded, it makes sense to evaluate the kind of alternative offerings described above.

The first point to make is that there will be very different customers for different types of service offerings and that even *within* the employer and employee markets there will be significant choices to be made. Just as firms now often insist on using different suppliers for different types of advice, so too it is likely that if they decided to do any business with a union they would want to have a single clear focus. Unions would therefore have to choose which approach they were going to make to a particular employer in the knowledge, say, that they could not present themselves credibly as a partner-in-change *and* a supplier of contracted-out labour.

Segmentation will also be the order of the day in the employee market. The service offerings described above (for example the representation service and the 'super broker' service) imply very different types of relationships with members and customers – to the extent indeed that there may well be resistance to taking them from the same supplier.

There is also an issue of *credibility* here. Some of the service offerings may be perfectly logical to describe but – take the 'lifetime partnership' approach to mobile workers, or the 'change partner' approach to employers – are far removed from what the potential customers expect unions to be able to deliver. The new service may sound attractive, but the gap between the new offering and the current practice and image of the potential supplier is so great that there is a big barrier to be overcome.

Unions would therefore have a long way to go to close the credibility gap. This is no different in kind, however, than the barriers faced – and successfully overcome – by many firms setting out to enter new markets: motor manufacturers as providers of credit cards and electronics companies as entertainment providers are but two recent examples. The key question is whether at the end of the day the potential supplier has the competence to deliver the service successfully.

The same considerations apply in respect of the economics of developing these sorts of service offerings. They are more individually based: slanted towards individual and semi-collective services rather than collective services. They also involve a much reduced element of employer subsidy since they are consciously designed to operate in a labour market where formal recognition of unions by employers is a much rarer event. To develop these sorts of service offerings therefore unions would have to raise more revenue by selling them at a higher price. On the basis of the London Business School analysis described at the beginning of this chapter this sounds at first like a recipe for disaster.

On closer reflection, however, some other considerations apply. Present levels of union subscription are kept low in large measure because they are implicitly tied to the collective bargaining model of union servicing. Union members consider in effect how much of their present pay packet it is worth sacrificing in order to improve the chance of increasing that pay packet – essentially a short term consumption decision. Other pricing principles apply to the offerings described above, however. The representation service, for example, implies something much more like the decision to buy insurance – or to join the AA. 'I might not need this service this year, indeed I very much hope that I never need it. But in an ever more uncertain world if I do need it I'll *really* need it so I'm prepared to pay a good premium for it.'

Some of the service offerings designed more with the employer market in mind have value-adding elements of consultancy advice to them, which again make room for more differentiated pricing in markets that can be quite readily segmented. As with conventional consultancies, however, (indeed perhaps even more so) there may well be conflict of interest issues that would limit the number of firms with whom it could work in this way.

Branding is another issue. It may well be that people are prepared to pay more for a particular service (the representation service for example) if it is presented under a new brand – separate from the union marque which is associated with the more commodity-like collective bargaining service.

Re-engineer the core processes

We have looked briefly at the revenue side of the economic balance sheet; what about the cost side? Unions have this in common with commercial organisations – they tie up a huge proportion of their resources in non-productive, non value-adding activities. Ask a union general secretary to describe his or her organisation and they will talk in terms of rulebooks and structure charts: of head office departments, of industrial or trade groups, of regions and area committees. In this they are like a general manager of a corporation who thinks of the organisation in terms of management hierarchies, functional departments and product groupings.

This is where re-engineering comes in. The key insight of the business process re-engineering literature[6] is that the economics of a business can be transformed by looking at it horizontally rather than vertically. In other words the starting point is to identify the core cross-cutting processes through which the business delivers to its customers and then to walk backwards through the organisation, re-engineering these core processes to simplify and strengthen them, and to cut out or redirect activities that do not add to, or even subtract from, the delivery of the core processes.

Unions are crying out for the application of this approach: even those unions with a well-earned reputation for comparative efficiency. What is needed is an approach that can unscramble the typical tangle of archaic structures and processes that mix up administrative and representative functions, that blur accountability, that perpetuate activities simply because they have always been carried out, and that tie up huge amounts of the organisation's talents and energies in inwardly-focused activities, rather than directing them outwards towards servicing the customers.

This is how a union might use re-engineering techniques to transform itself. First it would set about identifying its core processes. Setting aside the rulebook and the general secretary's structure chart, what are the key cross-cutting processes through which the union is going to deliver its service offerings? Likely candidates will be:

- Total sales process (ie from recruitment through to revenue collection).
- Individual customer service.
- Collective representation and negotiation.
- Asset management.
- Product and service development.
- Promotion and lobbying.

The next step would be work through each of these processes and see how they are currently carried out. How many changes of hands are involved? How many authorisation points? How many of the current participants actually add value to the process, and by how much? How long does it all take?

Next might come some benchmarking. What are the leading examples of good practice in the delivery of these processes – even from organisations in quite different businesses? What can be learned from them? What standards should be set?

Finally comes the re-engineering itself. How can the process be put back together again on a radically simplified and cleaner basis to deliver a service level that is up to leading external levels? And how can the resources liberated through this procedure be put into value-adding work delivering a higher level of service to customers?

Line up the structure

'Structure is a function of purpose', former TUC General Secretary, George Woodcock, used to say in reply to prescriptions for unions to embrace new organisational forms. Well, having derived its purpose through the stages of work described above, our 're-engineered' union can now look at its structure in a new light. The key questions it needs to address are whether it has got the resources and structures to deliver its redefined service offerings to the standard required by the re-engineered processes, and how it can reconcile the needs of its representative democracy with the achievements of better business results.

All other organisational considerations are secondary to these questions. And at their heart is a process, in effect, of competence mapping: what are the organisational competencies required to deliver the newly-defined purpose, to what extent does the organisation currently embrace these competencies, and what are the gaps?

This analysis provides the template for organisational responses. It might be that it produces a case for merger – linking up with an organisation whose competencies and gaps are complementary. It might on the contrary produce a case for 'unbundling' the union into self-standing units focused clearly on particular markets – specific employers, say, or specific types of employee.

More innovative responses might follow the approach being taken by the IPMS civil service union and a number of small employer-specific associations of professional staff. They are forming a federation that will leave each member association with its own brand and continuing to service its existing membership, but out-sourcing all the administrative functions in which they do not feel themselves to have a distinctive competence to what is in effect a separate service company – 'The Federation'.

We might also see the outlines of a new and valuable role for the Trades Union Congress in this approach. The Government's 1992 legislation in effect ended the 'Bridlington' rules that gave unions protected spheres of membership. By creating a free market in union membership it destroyed the TUC's principal purpose – policing Bridlington and thereby regulating inter-union relations. Without that role it is by no means clear what its overall locus is in the new scheme of things – other than as a general spokesman and lobbyist for issues that impinge on unions as a whole.

By analogy with other deregulated sectors we might envisage the TUC taking on a new kind of regulatory role – a sort of OFUNION! Experience in other sectors, however, has shown that attempts to combine regulatory powers with a role that is broadly that of lobbyist for the sector concerned are fraught with danger.

If we develop the idea of competence mapping, however, we might see the TUC's role redefined away from the idea of a *regulator* and towards that of a *market maker*. It would set itself the task of keeping fully abreast of all the latest developments in union competency. Which union has successfully dealt with the implications of a total quality or business process re-engineeering programme? Who is most up to date on the health hazards of office technology? Which union has developed the most innovative membership services? Who has displayed a real flair for public promotion? Where is the best brain on managing union assets? And so on.

The key asset of the TUC would therefore be an overall competence map of all of its affiliated unions. And the service that it would sell to unions would be a brokerage. It would help unions fill the gaps in their own organisations by buying in – either permanently or for a specific time and purpose – the best available from other unions. It might play this role in a low-key way – providing the players with information and letting them get on with making their own deals. Or it might be a more active agent: buying and selling, filling gaps in the overall picture either by developing the required competence in-house or by buying it in from a completely external source. Whichever approach was taken it would at least allow the TUC to assert more confidently its relevance to the modern labour relations scene. It would also cut with the grain of the bold and imaginative 'relaunch' of the TUC undertaken by new General Secretary, John Monks, which has been associated with a radical overhaul of the organisation and deployment of the TUC's resources.

CONCLUSIONS

The content of this chapter, and indeed its language and terminology, may make trade union readers feel uncomfortable. Some may feel that it is excessively focused on the business aspects of trade unionism and insufficiently attentive to the political, representative role that unions have to perform, which makes them preoccupied with the need to balance a large number of often conflicting roles. So be it. Perhaps they need to feel some more discomfort. For the last 15 years many unions seem to have settled for a future of comfortable decline. They have created a culture of managed dcfcat.

The purpose of this chapter has been to run the same analytical eye over unions that would be used to assess any business that had seen a collapse in demand in its core markets. The union response to that collapse has been frankly inadequate. What would a business analyst say of organisations that had spent their energy on internal battles rather than winning new customers? That had produced no significant new product over a period of over a decade when demand for its established product had halved? That had fiddled with new initiatives and reorganisations but had evolved no distinctive and new organisational response to a transformed marketplace? It's not hard to imagine the answer.

The argument of this book has been that there is still a case for trade unionism in the radically-changed labour markets of the 1990s. In the right circumstances trade unions can add value for employer and employee and make the whole market work better. But it has to be said that as yet trade unions have done precious little to live up to this opportunity. The opening is there, but as with any other business organisation there is no God-given right to succeed. The detail of the ideas in this chapter will not be right for all unions at all times. But unless the challenge is addressed on the scale and with the seriousness implied here – and indeed with the seriousness that a fully commercial concern would display – managed decline may end up as the likeliest prospect.

References

1. Willman, P, Morris, T and Aston, B (1993) *Union Business: Trade Union Organisation and financial Reform in the Thatcher Years*, Cambridge University Press, Cambridge, p 51
2. Ibid. p 214
3. Bassett, P and Cave, A (1993) *All For One: the Future of Trade Unions*, Fabian Society, London
4. Handy, C (1990) *The Age of Unreason*, Arrow Books, London, pp 146–67
5. Bassett, P and Cave, A (1993) *All For One: the Future of Trade Unions*, Fabian Society, London
6. Hammer, M and Champy, J (1993) *Reengineering the Corporation*, Nicholas Brealey Publishing, London

CHAPTER 9
Conclusions

THE AREA IN QUESTION

Successive chapters of this book have taken us on a rather eclectic voyage. We have examined new ideas and theories drawn from a diverse range of subjects and disciplines. We have stood back in order to look at the big picture, and we have zoomed in to look at specific examples of real life practice. Throughout, however, the area in question has been the following: *in a time of great economic and social upheaval, what has fundamentally changed in the way in which employers seek to manage the relationship with those whom they employ?*

The eclecticism is needed because this issue is claimed as its own by different disciplines (industrial relations, human resource management, organisational behaviour, and so on) and indeed different institutions, which typically fail to communicate with one another over the walls erected by their different traditions, theoretical roots, imagery and paradigms in order to reach a shared understanding. Hence the metaphor, established in Chapter 1, of trying to turn a prism in order to look afresh at the area of common ground, and at the subsidiary questions within the principal one:

- Are businesses now better organised, more efficiently managed, and more successful as a result of changes in the way in which they manage people?
- Are labour markets working more efficiently as a result of the dismantling of many of the institutions and regulations which previously governed them?
- Are employers any better, after a decade and more of managerial revolution, at managing relationships with large numbers of employees?
- Has the renewed stress on individualism, and the down-rating

of collective approaches to the management of employees, improved the position of people at work?

∎ Has a management agenda which is now heavy with concepts such as 'gaining commitment', 'empowerment', 'flexibility' and 'self directed teamwork' made the world of work a less alienating and more participative place for workforces, or is it rather, in the words of the song, a case of 'meet the new boss – the same as the old boss'?

The approach taken in looking at these and other related questions has been heavily UK centred. At a time when key decisions of business strategy have been increasingly taken on an international plane, this may seem strange – even a weakness. The reality is, however, that this sphere – the content, style and conduct of employee relations – seems to have remained resolutely national in its focus. This is not to say that cases and trends from other countries offer no learning or insights: they clearly do. Nor is it to presume that domestic employee relations will be untouched by decisions on a company's global production strategy. Still less is it to ignore the impact on UK employee relations from the activities of incoming firms who bring other traditions and styles with them – whether, say, from North America or from Asia – or from the legislative and regulatory work of the European Community.

The point is rather that these external influences represent variations around a solid central theme that is made up for the most part of national custom, practice and culture. As we have seen, the realm of employee relations is essentially reactive. It is concerned with gaining acceptance, agreement, even commitment to decisions that arise from corporate business strategy. Not surprisingly then the organisations that seek to take a supra-national approach to the management of employment relationships are rare. Typically a more tactical approach prevails: what is needed to get a particular workforce, employed in a specific locality and operating under the provisions of that country's framework of law and practice, to go along with a particular decision or strategy?

Largely stripped of international considerations, then, the field of employee relations can give a vivid and accurate account of the state at any one time of British managerial culture, and in particular of the prevailing attitude towards the value assigned to people in the productive process.

In this concluding chapter, therefore, we will set down the account as we have found it in earlier chapters. First we will look at the light that we can shed on some issues of controversy and debate – on the nature and definition of strategic HRM for example, or on the reality behind the rhetoric of 'empowerment'. Then we will focus more specifically and practically on the employee relations scene. What is left of the field of industrial relations as it was understood until the 1980s? What are the dominant strains in the new scene, and what trends can we foresee for the next decade?

Finally we will draw up a balance sheet of the changes that have occurred in the field of employee relations over the period we have examined and assess the extent to which long-remarked weaknesses in the way in which business managed its relationships with its employees have been put right.

SHEDDING SOME LIGHT

At various points in this book we have encountered a number of issues that are the subject of debate among commentators and observers. This is the place to pull together the threads and to add what we can to those debates. There are three areas in particular in which there are points to be made.

Is there a new 'model' for UK employee relations?

At issue here is whether, having moved in a decisive way from a fairly clear established 'system' of employee relations, we have moved to another equally well-defined system, and, if we have not, whether it matters.

Have the pressures and circumstances of the last 15 years – the changes in industrial structure, in technology, in the composition of the workforce, and in legislation – combined to create not just a series of adjustments and tactical responses but a lasting *shift* in behaviour, institutions, rules and expectations? Have we, to use the key signifiers, moved from a world of collectivism to one of individualism; from one which respected a plurality of different influences and voices to a unitarist one; from the world of industrial relations, with its emphasis on the regulation of the employment relationship whatever the business context, to one of HRM, with its stress on achieving 'fit' between the management of people and the requirements of business strategy?

The considerations of earlier chapters have led us to the view that it is easier to see the move away from one system than a clear, widespread embracing of a new model. Certainly the old industrial relations paradigm has lost ground across whole swathes of the economy; the attempt to argue that it is merely keeping its head down waiting for better times simply doesn't stand up. Yet, outside the relatively small number of greenfield sites, where a whole new integrated employee relations philosophy has been imported wholesale, what we can see instead is something which looks much more like a patchwork quilt, or something even messier, than a complete new system.

True, there is a greater stress than before on the individual and on managing employment relationships on a more individualistic basis. There is also a greater impatience with the notion of formally consulting and negotiating over change, and a bigger emphasis on leadership, briefing and winning commitment, all of which can be interpreted as a movement away from pluralism in the workplace and towards a more unitarist philosophy. And yet throughout much of the economy, the institutions of collective industrial relations remain more or less intact, albeit that they are used less frequently and within a more confined remit. Elsewhere, as we have seen, there is a conscious 'dualism', as organisations operate in a more individualistic and proactive way towards their staff while keeping the old ways alive, either as a fallback or because it makes it easier to win workforce acquiescence.

If, however, there is not a clear new employee relations 'model' to replace neatly the old 'British system' of industrial relations, there is at least a common and reasonably consistent thrust, and that is about managerial power. The frontier of control has been rolled back to a significant degree so that issues, groups and features which previously were subject to a considerable degree of joint regulation are now firmly in the field of management discretion.

Moreover, that discretion is being exercised much further down the line of management structures than ever before and much closer to the workforce itself, as employers have sought to internalise their labour markets and cease 'importing' from the outside world, or even from another business unit or from the head office of their own organisation. In consequence the workforce is finding itself much more *actively* managed than hitherto, and in many, though by no means all, cases, more productively managed as well. That is the distinguishing hallmark of the new shape of British employee relations: more managerial power over employees and a more active use of that power. The next key question then is whether managers are using this new found power to forge a closer integration between the management of people and the strategic requirements of the business.

What about strategic HRM?

In a way this is shorthand for asking how managers and firms have used the greater degree of discretion that they have, in managing the relationship with their employees. The concept of strategic HRM implies, as we saw in Chapter 4, that the devolution of responsibility for people management down the line will take place within a strategic framework that links business needs with the components of the human resource cycle: resourcing, performance management, reward, development and so on. Business needs, in other words, drive human resource strategies, and HRM is 'strategic' because it is about achieving a fit between what happens on the ground and the requirements of the business, now and in the future.

The concept of strategic HRM therefore implies that managers are not only more free and more active, but that they are business-driven in their management of people – not just in respect of the short term but over a long-term perspective too. They are value-driven too – navigating by the compass of corporate mission, values and culture in the absence of prescriptive manuals or central personnel departments; and they are developmental – seeking to ensure that the organisation realises the competitive edge that is available from their 'greatest asset'. Well, are they?

The message from earlier chapters is that the picture on the ground is of a much less strategic pattern of behaviour and a far greater degree of opportunism than the model would imply. In practice the 'greatest asset' has continued to be seen as the single most entrenched source of cost – one whose short-term performance has to be driven very hard and whose long-term development can, for the most part, wait. True there are some significant exceptions to this picture – organisations whose practice undoubtedly falls squarely within the definition of strategic HRM. They are, however, few on the ground. And there is about them something which appears to many practising managers to be, well, not quite the done thing.

Less rare is a rather opportunistic adoption of individual aspects of HRM – especially in respect of the employment of managerial staff. Moreover the rapid spread of some of these components of strategic HRM, notably performance management and performance related pay, has helped the process noted above – of taking areas of the employment relationship out of the realm of joint determination and into the area of managerial discretion. These elements can be portrayed as strategic in the sense that they seek to align the objectives of the individual with the pursuit of business goals and to reward only behaviour and activities that support the attainment of these goals. They also happen to provide a far greater degree of management leverage over the behaviour of the employee and their remuneration.

The contrast here is with old-style piecework systems in which pay was linked to the volume of output and which were open to workgroup manipulation of production and to the interventions of well-informed shop stewards. With performance related pay the manager retains control over the judgement of whether or not an individual employee has performed satisfactorily and there is little, if any, room for the intervention of the shop steward.

Our argument then is that while many of the structures and employment relationships embraced by the notion of 'industrial relations' have been dismantled, neutered or bypassed, they have not been straightforwardly replaced by a new model. Full blown instances of strategic HRM remain few and far between. On the other hand there is a consistent trend at work: the growth in managerial power and discretion. So, if we are right to say that managers have a lot more power and influence but that they are not often using it in a more strategic way, the next question concerns how they are using it. And in particular whether they are behaving in the ways predicted by the new models of management reviewed in earlier chapters.

New model management?

The issue here concerns the use of power and freedom. As we have seen, the emerging model of a successful and high performing manager is that of a changed man or woman. The paradigm has shifted: from a concern with command and control to an emphasis on empowerment, facilitation and mentoring; from a view of people as costs to a recognition of their value as an asset; from policeman to coach; from the maintainers of hierarchy to the creators of space for self-directing work teams, and so on. Many of the features that were previously seen as impediments to this paradigm shift have been removed – by the same forces that have so drastically redrawn the map of industrial relations: the emergence of flexible production technologies, information systems that make effective delegation of accountability a reality, the internalisation of labour markets, the weakening of extra-firm institutions, and the more subtle but crucial growth in the social legitimacy of the use of managerial authority.

And yet we are left with the sense that the changes that we have seen fall far short of the new model for management. Partly this may be because much of the visible change has been at the rhetorical level – the level of the management conference, the corporate mission statement, the management consultant's presentation. This is also the faddish level, where fashionable phrases are the small change of managerial talk – not signifying any lasting change in practice but representing a vague hope that one day we might find a better way to cope with the stressful business of managing large numbers of people.

John le Carre has the quintessentially lugubrious George Smiley putting the point in the following terms:[1]

> He had watched Whitehall's skirts go up, and come down again, her belts being loosened, tightened, loosened. He had been the witness, or victim – or even reluctant prophet – of such spurious cults as lateralism, parallelism, separatism, operational devolution and now ... of integration. Each new fashion had been hailed as a panacea: 'Now we shall vanquish, now the machine will work!' Each had gone out with a whimper, leaving behind it the familiar English muddle.

Too cynical a view? Perhaps. But as we saw in Chapters 5 and 6, when we look closely at how large numbers of employers have been using their newly expanded freedoms we find a rather depressing picture. Certainly we can see a shift of approach. There is clear evidence of a much more *active* management of the employment relationship – whether through performance management systems, new forms of work organisation, or changed approaches to supervision. This has tended also to represent a much *harder* management of people. It may be argued that this has been necessary: that after a period of lax, even invisible, management there needed to be a general tightening up – more 'grip', a harder drive, and so on.

The trouble with this is twofold. First, it means that there is a huge gulf between the rhetoric of many organisations – which is firmly based on the new model of the empowering, sharing and high-trust firm – and the reality of the employment and management relationships within it which, to use the old distinction, is much more 'work to live' than 'live to work'. As one senior executive was heard to remark: 'Most examples of empowerment in Britain have been about shafting employees – dumping our problems on them, and expecting them to do six hours' extra work a day.'[2] The result is an understandably high level of employee cynicism and a reluctance to take managerial initiatives too seriously – on the basis that there will probably be another one along, together with a new chief executive, in a few minutes.

Second, viewed in macro terms, the result of all this represents something of a failure on the part of British management. If we accept the argument that in global markets marked by unprecedented speed of change, the successful firm will need to mobilise all its intelligence and resourcefulness through an empowering, facilitating, high-trust relationship with its employees, then the evidence of Chapters 5 and 6 is fairly damning. It reveals that given an unprecedented opportunity to reshape its relationship with its employees, most of British industry has grabbed instinctively and energetically for the low-trust 'command and control' model of yesteryear. In doing so they have participated energetically in a trend that is by no means restricted to the UK: what Richard Pascale[3] sees as the development of a 'peasantry' created by companies shedding workers whose skills are not seen as critical to their competitive advantage. 'There's a very large chunk of humanity with very limited prospects. I don't see any light at the end of the tunnel. There's going to be a great many people in this pool.'

Moreover within the area of employment that remains after the 'stripping out' of those who are no longer core to the business, there is another more basic sense in which the emerging picture is depressing. The data cited in Chapter 5 from the Government's Workplace Industrial Relations Survey suggests that, given new powers and freedoms to operate in a less regulated labour market, and with less interference from trade unions, many employers have responded by creating employment conditions that are low and getting lower. The growing incidence of unfair dismissal, declining standards of safety at work, higher incidence of discriminatory treatment – all these have become prominent features of the increasing segment of the economy that is unregulated either by employment protection law or by the presence of effective trade unions. None of these features have anything much to do with the creation of long-term competitive advantage. They owe much more to arbitrariness and a narrowly 'macho' model of successful management than to any convincing model of what a high performing organisation looks like.

Against this backdrop, the most convincing argument for some pluralism in employment relations, and more specifically for a role for independent trade unionism, is therefore the evidence of managerial behaviour itself. If that is how a large body of managers behave when granted new freedoms and powers over their employees, then there is indeed a strong case – micro and macro – for some effective checks and balances in the system.

THE CASE FOR PLURALISM

Previous chapters have chronicled the rapid erosion of the institutions and processes that previously supported the pluralist system of industrial relations in this country – pluralist in the sense of giving institutional weight and legitimacy to the expression of an alternative point of view to that of the employer within the organisation. The sharp fall in trade union membership has been charted, as has the decline in the scope and coverage of the institutions of collective bargaining and the content of the agreements reached through it. The steady and continuous tilting of the legal balance in favour of employers has also been set out.

If on the basis of this account we were asked 'what's left of industrial relations', the answer would have to be 'not much'. The image would be of an island in a largely hostile sea; an island moreover in which for the most part nothing very active or positive was happening, bar perhaps a few isolated cases of innovation and progressive thinking. The question then is whether this matters at all.

We have come across three arguments for saying that it does matter. The first is an argument that says that unregulated labour markets do not always produce the best of outcomes in the best of all possible worlds – for the individual, the firm or the economy as a whole. This is the argument that says that there are 'externalities' and 'public goods': outcomes that would strengthen the system as a whole and the individual firms within it but which will never be in the short-term economic interest of the individual firm to produce by itself. Outcomes such as a workforce with a high level of transferable skills, not just skills whose application is limited to the one firm, or a healthier workforce, or safer workplaces, or a reduced level of discrimination on grounds of sex or race.

All these are outcomes that will tend to be eroded rather than enhanced in deregulated labour markets, in which employers are constantly seeking to internalise their employee relations, to cut the links with external structures or comparators and to reduce the cost of employment.

In this argument trade unions can provide a counter-balance to the internalising forces – building linkages and enabling comparisons with other sectors, thereby facilitating the transfer of skills and the levelling up of good industrial practices. Indeed it might even be argued that, by acting to widen the skill base and thereby reducing supply side bottlenecks, the pluralism of trade unionism can act to diminish the aggregate inflationary effect of a labour market in which internalisation has been taken too far, resulting in excessive barriers between firms and extensive shortages of particular skills.

Unions, moreover, have a strong internal representative dynamic which makes them the natural champions of healthier and safer work, and of a greater equalisation of opportunities between sexes and races. Under the right circumstances therefore effective trade unions can make labour markets function more effectively. That is certainly the argument of those who have analysed the role of unions in, for example, post-war Germany, Austria and Scandinavia.

The second argument for pluralism is best represented by the Californian car plant described in Chapter 6. The transformation of the 'worst factory in the world' into a plant that matched and even exceeded Japanese levels of productivity and quality was achieved through a programme of change that actively encouraged the retention and involvement of the union representatives who had previously been associated with much that was negative and harmful in the plant's earlier industrial relations.

The logic behind this approach fits very closely with the overall argument of this concluding chapter. The adoption of new working practices and managerial systems, it was argued, gave the firm's managers an unprecedented degree of potential power over their employees. At the same time the real breakthroughs that the company needed in productivity and quality would only be forthcoming if the workforce trusted the company enough to 'let go' and radically change their attitudes and behaviour. This trust would not materialise if there remained a lingering suspicion that managers might use their new, less-constrained power in a hostile or oppressive way. The continued existence of the union, and indeed the active involvement in the change programme of its most prominent and forthright representatives, was therefore a sign that the company did not intend to give its managers a 'free run' to use their newly enhanced powers against the workforce. It was therefore an important condition for removing that suspicion and creating the trust that was needed in order to make space for the required shift in attitudes and behaviours.

Here we have an argument for pluralism that puts it not as an alternative to the pursuit of the goals that the more unencumbered managers of recent years have been striving for but, indeed, as a condition for success in that pursuit. Pluralism helps create trust, which helps shift behaviour, and thus performance.

The third argument for pluralism is the most basic and traditional one. It is not an argument about the achievement of employer objectives but rather one about the protection of employee rights: about basic fairness. This is the argument that says that the growing power of employers *vis à vis* their employees shows strong signs of being abused. The symptoms of this abuse can be found in the growing incidence of unfair treatment of people at work, of discrimination, unsocial patterns of work, increased insecurity and higher stress, and a general concern at the emergence of a low-paid, under-skilled, unmotivated 'underclass' in society.

The argument can be made at various levels: that this emerging picture is symptomatic of an economy that is taking a wrong turn, trying to compete on a low-cost basis just as the previously low-cost nations are rapidly coming up market in terms of skills and quality; or that it militates against the progressive, quality employer who is trying to compete on the basis of improving the standards of production; or simply that this is not a development that a civilised society should tolerate.

However the argument is pitched, the implication is the same. Trade unionism can provide a pluralistic, counterbalancing constraint against the exercise of managerial powers that have damaging consequences. Industrial pluralism therefore is proposed in the same way as its political counterpart – as a system of checks and balances against the abuse of executive power.

THE GAP

Here then we have a set of arguments for the pluralism in employee relations that became deeply unfashionable in the 1980s. At the same time we have seen that the forces that helped produce that shift in approach in the 1980s are still at large and still powerful.

Foremost among them is the simple fact that the overwhelming force of managerial opinion remains hostile to sharing its new-found power with the very institutions from which it so painfully wrested that power. Remember the claim of the manager, quoted in Chapter 6, that his colleagues would look upon him with baffled incomprehension if he were to suggest even the most minimal involvement of employee representatives in discussions about company policy. Like so many managers, they had moved beyond hostility towards pluralism and on to astonishment that it should ever have been contemplated as a contribution to their business.

The second factor is the failure of the trade unions themselves to come to terms with the changed market conditions and to redefine their roles in ways that would enable them to protect and advance their members' interests within the context of contributing to the competitive success of the organisations that employ them.

In Chapter 8 we have described the scale of the 're-engineering' that trade unions need to carry out on themselves, and provided some pointers to how this process could be undertaken. Meanwhile the continuing weakness and apparent aimlessness of much of the trade union movement serves to undermine the case for pluralism ('you mean you want us to do business with *this* lot?').

And finally of course there is no sign of any reversal in the one-way flow of legislation that has so fundamentally re-weighted the balance of power between unions and employers – taking away virtually all the sources of leverage that unions once had with which to try and force their way to the table. It looked for a while at the turn of the decade as if the social legislation of the European Union might – through measures such as the European Company Statute and the Social Charter – provide a counterweight to UK domestic legislation and give unions avenues of influence to replace those that had been taken away. That now seems to be a false hope, or alarm, depending on your point of view. The framework of UK law is therefore going to continue for the foreseeable future to promote deregulated labour markets, individualistic employment contracts and unitarist managerial philosophies.

The gap then is between the potential contribution that a greater degree of pluralism could make, both to the performance of organisations and to the conditions of working life within them, and the powerful forces that prevent that potential from being realised. Should we worry about this gap, or should we simply shrug and dismiss it as one of those things that we can't really do anything about?

In order to answer this, let's look at the rough balance sheet of the changes of the last decade and a half as they have affected the employment relationship.

■ It is now much easier to hire, deploy, promote and train staff in line with business needs – *and* there is an increased likelihood that these decisions will be laced with a higher degree of discrimination, arbitrariness and perceived unfairness.

■ There is far more scope to reward and promote individuals on the basis of their individual merit rather than the length of their service or some other rule-based criterion – *and* there is more chance that the 'awkward customer' – the creative individual who doesn't conform – will come under pressure to fit in or move out.

■ There is a stronger emphasis on building the skills and competences that the business needs locally, rather than on meeting industry wide standards – *and* there is a corresponding reduction in the interchangeability of skills across organisational and sectoral boundaries.

■ There has been a massive decentralisation of decision-making over all aspects of employment to line managers – *and* this has put more power in the hands of managers who have to a considerable degree been found sadly lacking in terms of 'people skills'.

■ It is now much easier to sever the seemingly irrelevant links with 'outside' bodies – whether they are trade unions, employers' associations, training bodies or whatever – and to focus the attention of staff on the needs of the core business – *and* there is a pretty patchy track record in terms of using this new space to build stronger, more trusting relationships between the business and its employees.

And so on. What we seem to have therefore is a classic case of suboptimisation. On the one hand the ground has been cleared for employers to follow a far more unitarist path than hitherto – building structures, systems and approaches which meet Gareth Morgan's definition:[4] 'An organisation which places emphasis on the achievement of common objectives, (and which is) viewed as being united under the umbrella of common goals and striving towards their achievement in the manner of a well-integrated team.'

And yet, with some spectacular exceptions, organisations have shown themselves to lack the skills and attitudes needed to unlock the trust on the part of their people, which is the secret of getting real business value out of a unitarist approach.

Meanwhile, in large areas of the economy, an ambivalence remains. Employers retain the formal structures of pluralist relationships – union recognition, consultative committees, collective agreements and so on – but do nothing to make them more integral to the business. As a result, at a time when the way in which employees are managed and involved is of unprecedented importance, what were the chief vehicles for regulating these relationships are now relegated to the margins of corporate concern and little or nothing is done to get more out of them.

CONCLUDING POINTS

A gap is an uncomfortable place to end a book. It's all very well spotting mismatches and highlighting contradictions but it isn't very helpful to practical people. So to end this survey of trends and analysis of changes here are three sets of observations which are put forward as pointers to possible ways forward. They share these common assumptions about the future:

■ That the 'balance of power' in the employment relationship has been shifted in the employer's favour, and will remain so for the foreseeable future.
■ That, in particular, employers will continue to enjoy an unprecedented degree of choice over the basis on which they structure and organise their relationships with their employees.
■ That employers will find a relative lack of consensus concerning the basis or 'model' around which they should exercise that choice.

Against that background the first concluding observation concerns *theory*. It is a striking truth that the UK imports the lion's share of its management theory. Perhaps this is a reflection of the John Bull-like belief that management is essentially a practical matter best left to practical chaps; but whatever the cause, the fact is that most of the developments in management thinking recorded in this book – and which, as we have seen, have had a strong impact on the real world – have not been home-grown. For the most part they have been imported in popularised form from the US, with some noteworthy twists from Japan – and with Europe being notable by its absence.

The point here is not to decry the validity of ideas because of their origin but instead to emphasise the importance of some of the key assumptions that lie behind these ideas, which often are not made explicit and which can materially affect the degree to which they can be imported, installed and beneficially switched on in a 'turnkey' fashion.

Much of the 'empowerment' and 'human resource management' thinking, for example, with which many British managements have sought to change radically their employee relations, originates in the US. In that setting it has running through it a set of strong assumptions about social and employment mobility, inalienable individual rights and democratic 'citizenship' in its widest sense, that has only a weak echo in the more class-ridden and hierarchical employment and social structures of the typical British institution. Importing the techniques of HRM, therefore, but applying them in organisations managed according to a less democratic spirit inevitably creates a distinctive and somewhat more oppressive form of unitarism.

The counterpart to this point concerns the danger of throwing out the benefit of some of the thinking and institution-building that had previously taken place in a specifically UK context in order to create space to lever into place the imported 'new thinking'.

As we have recalled in this chapter a recurring criticism of British management has been that it is, on any significant scale, singularly bad at managing relationships with people. This may well be largely due to the relative lack of seriousness with which management – and therefore the skills that it requires – has been taken in our national culture, and also the impact over time of our debilitating class system which so inhibits trust and honest exchange between people at different levels in organisations. This weakness created a vacuum and into that vacuum grew a set of institutions and processes – trade unions, negotiated agreements, 'custom and practice' and so on – which were in effect a pragmatic and home-grown response to the flaw at the heart of British management. They might not have been ideal, but they did help keep the show on the road: providing a basis on which large-scale employment relationships could be managed in a relatively low-trust but reasonably well accepted manner.

A problem now arises for British managers who have successfully rid themselves of institutions and processes that they had come to see as a burden, but have not done anything positive to fill the vacuum. Can they change their own behaviour and attitudes in ways that would raise the level of trust between themselves and those they manage, and thereby gain a real shift in performance within the less regulated employment relationships that they have now created?

This leads straight on to the second observation which concerns *managerial skills*. As we have noted at several points, a high proportion of change initiatives are found to fail – or at least to deliver less than the anticipated return – because of the failure to achieve significant shifts in behaviour. This in turn is often laid at the door of inadequate people-management skills on the part of British managers.

A useful index of this is the flourishing (some would say belatedly flourishing) market in training for managers in the skills – coaching, mentoring, giving honest feedback etc – required to implement successfully a performance management system. It is often the middle management level, who interface most directly with the front-line workforce, who feel most discomfort at the introduction of proper performance management simply because they have always been insulated from real dialogue with their staff by a mass of intervening personnel procedures, union agreements, and other bureaucratic devices. Now they, and their lack of people-management skills, are exposed for the first time because they actually have to talk to their staff about what is expected of them, what support they are going to give them, and how well they are doing.

There are two possible reactions to this state of affairs. One is that it may well be that by knocking down the artificial barriers between managers and staff and exposing them directly in this way managers will be made more accountable for the way in which they manage people, that their skills will be sharpened up, and that, indeed, a higher level of demand will be generated for training and support for managers so that they do develop new and more effective ways of doing business with their people.

The other reaction is that, in workplaces where that demand is not met, where managers feel that they will be judged by their willingness to take 'tough' decisions with their staff, and where the level of managerial skill was not terribly high to begin with, the effect of this development – from the point of view of those on the receiving end of it – will be, as they used to say in the Westerns, like giving guns to the Indians.

The third, and concluding, observation is that from every standpoint, and no matter how unfashionable it may be, there is a strong case for the evolving patchwork quilt of employee relations to include a sizable pluralist element: one that rests on the recognition of independent trade unions, as long as these unions are *worth* doing business with – worth it for employers and worth it for employees.

The precise case for this element, and therefore the form that it takes, will vary from sector to sector, from firm to firm. In some cases, such as those caricatured slightly in the previous paragraph, the case will rest on the simple social justice point of putting some constraint upon the exercise of an overweening power that may do serious harm to citizens who deserve better.

Elsewhere the case may revolve around the efficiency gains that may follow from involving trusted workforce representatives in a process of radical change, giving individual employees the confidence to 'let go', secure in the knowledge that in thereby taking a risk and trying something new their trust will not be abused. Elsewhere again the case for pluralism will rest on the existence of economic 'externalities' – recognition that however far it devolves and de-layers, an organisation cannot resolve all its difficulties by building a wall around itself and seeking to internalise all aspects of its labour markets. In these circumstances the organisation needs bridges and well-managed relationships with the outside world, and independent trade unions can contribute to this process.

At a national level these sentiments were echoed by a *Financial Times* editorial that concluded its survey of the continuing role and potential contribution of trade unions with the comment that:[5] 'Unions are uniquely well-placed to voice the concerns of people at work in national discussions on workplace matters such as health and safety, employment law and pensions. If the TUC did not exist, a government might have to create a surrogate to represent such interests in the future.'

In just the same way, the argument of this book has been that if unions continue to fade from the scene, employers may well end up having to invent something to help them in the area which has typically seen them at their least effective – the management of their relationships with their employees. Given that this is so, it will often make more sense for them to swallow their distaste and do, or continue doing, business with the genuine, rather than the surrogate, article.

And here's the final rub. As we have seen in the previous chapter this presents unions in Britain with a tremendous challenge. The cards are stacked against them and they have only a few plays that they can make. The rules of the new game are, however fixed, and to make something of it unions are going to have to 'reinvent' themselves with all the energy and commitment of a General Electric or a Xerox Corporation. If they don't then they may be a matter of history within a working lifetime. If they do, they can contribute something to the development of the British economy, without which business performance will probably be lower than it need be, and working life for many thousands will be more unpleasant and less rewarding than it ought to be.

References

1. le Carre, J (1980) *Smiley's People*, Hodder and Stoughton, Sevenoaks, p 138
2. Lorenz, C 'A New World That May Be Some Time Coming', *Financial Times*, 3 December 1993
3. Pascale, R 'Turning Doers Back Into Thinkers', *Independent on Sunday*, 28 November 1993
4. Morgan, G (1986) *Images of Organisation*, Sage, London, p 188
5. Lorenz, C 'Moving on at the TUC', *Financial Times*, 27 April 1993

Index

deindustrialisation 28
deregulation 14, 30–1
de-skilling 32
devolution 14, 30
diversification 30
Dock Labour Scheme 106
Donovan Commission 95–6, 97
drivers
  performance appraisal 157–8
  strategic 51–3, 142
dualism 126, 132

Eisenstat, E 65
Electrical Power Engineers
  Association 162
employee
  commitment 82–3
  dismissal 102–3
  empowerment 128–31, 208
employee relations 18–19
  and change 66–7, 117–18
  and markets 51–2
  and organisational structure
    53–68, 195–6
  effect of legislation on 92,
    100–115
  employer-led 121 *et seq*
  see also human relations
    management; industrial
    relations
employers, choices for 19–22,
  108–10, 116–39
employment
  contract 27 *see also* contracts
  female 27, 35, 36, 102
  part-time 27, 36
  trends 27–45
Employment Acts 100–3, 105
Empowered Manager, The 130
empowerment 128–31, 206, 208
enterprise unionism 175–7

European Union 92, 107, 171,
  193, 203

federalism 37
Financial Management
  Initiative 31
financial services sector 28
firms *see* organisations
flexibility 14, 33–40
  employee 78–80, 110, 119,
    182
Ford, employee projects 82,
  127, 136, 176
Fowler, Alan 44, 75, 86
Fox, Alan 67
Freeman, R 130

GCH 104
GMB 156, 165, 169, 171, 172
Goold, Michael 58–60
'greenfield' sites 109, 125
Guest, David 59, 76–8, 83

Handy, Charles 36, 37, 67, 180
Harvard Business Review 65,
  137
health and safety 181, 200–1
Hewlett Packard 83
HRM *see* human resource
  management
human resource management
  16–18, 40–3, 61, 70–90,
  124, 127, 128, 206
  and trade unions 76, 79–80,
  89
  'hard' 77, 87, 119, 125
  'soft' 77
  strategic 83–5, 194–7

IBM 82–3
Incomes Data Services 35, 79
industrial action 102, 106, 162